HIRING ON PURPOSE

hiring on purpose

how the Y Scouts method
is revolutionizing the
search for leaders

max hansen & brian mohr

HIRING ON PURPOSE

How the Y Scouts Method Is Revolutionizing the Search for Leaders

ISBN 978-1-5445-0203-8 *Paperback*

978-1-5445-0204-5 *Ebook*

To all of our clients who've trusted us with their most critical leadership hires, to all of the leaders who've opened their hearts and minds to our unique search process, and to the entire Y Scouts crew, both past and present, this book would not be possible without your willingness to challenge the status quo and help us transform the way people and companies connect to work that matters.

From Max:
To my wife, Bryna, and our kids, Raiden, Maxwell, Kyla, Bradley, and baby Monroe, thank you for continuous support and love in everything I do. I would never have pulled this off without you.

From Brian:
To my wife, Jackie, and our daughters, Taylor and Riley, thank you for inspiring me to continue learning, growing, and serving others. I love you more than words can tell.

Contents

Introduction

Who Should Not Read This Book

Should you read this book? Maybe not.

You should not read this book if you think hiring is a chore instead of an opportunity.

You should not read this book if you think the way you've always gone about hiring is going to keep working in the changing world of business.

You should not read this book if you believe that the minute you put out a job posting, the right candidates should come begging you for a job.

You should not read this book if you think you know

everything there is to know about hiring, and no one can teach you anything new.

You should not read this book if you think that just because you have a title, you are a leader.

You should not read this book if you believe the only reason a company exists is to make money.

You should not read this book if you believe people are interchangeable parts.

You should not read this book if you think engaging people's hearts and souls in their work does not matter.

You should not read this book if you don't believe that the word "purpose" has meaning in every business, everywhere—in the most rarified executive suites and on the most repetitive factory floors.

You should not read this book if you believe that people should do a good job just because you pay them well.

You should not read this book if you believe people are lucky to work for you.

You should not read this book if you are an asshole and plan on staying an asshole.

And finally, you should not read this book if you think hiring is easy, doesn't take a whole lot of resources, and can be delegated to lowly underlings.

Because—excuse our French—hiring leaders is fucking difficult. It just is. And anyone who doesn't recognize this difficulty will not succeed.

WHO *SHOULD* READ THIS BOOK AND WHY

You should read this book if you believe people are the only sustainable competitive advantage in today's ever-changing business world.

You should read this book if your company needs a new direction, and you have to find someone capable of discovering, articulating, and moving you in that direction.

You should read this book if you are a board member, a CEO, a COO, a VP, a recruiter, an HR person, or anyone with the need and authority to hire leaders—but you end up, over and over, with the wrong people.

You should read this book if you have no idea why that keeps happening to you.

You should read this book if you're a person with a big title but you're not an asshole.

Or, of course, if you are but want to *stop* being an asshole.

THE VERY BIG MISTAKE

Let's start with the fact that even smart people with lots of resources make catastrophic hiring errors all the time. Usually because they're hungry. In fact, we know a scary bedtime story that illustrates this point perfectly.

Once upon a time, a group of bears grew very hungry. So hungry, they made a very big mistake.

They were the Chicago Bears, they were hungry for a Super Bowl, and the mistake was named Jay Cutler.

As everyone in football knows, to build a team worthy of a Super Bowl, you must start with a great quarterback. The quarterback does more than handle the ball in every play—he's almost always looked upon as the leader of the team.

Like many organizations, the Bears had been struggling for years to find a truly amazing quarterback who would lead their team forward, inspire his fellow players with his example, and work hand in hand with the coaching staff to drive the club to excellence.

In 2009, the very hungry Bears looked at the resumes

of all the available candidates. They wanted a proven winner, and one resume really stood out.

Jay Cutler had really kicked ass in college: 710 career completions for 8,697 yards and 59 touchdowns, along with 453 rushing attempts for 1,256 yards and 17 touchdowns. Pundits had tabbed Cutler as the best available quarterback in the draft, and he'd been nominated for lots of awards.

When he left school in 2006, Cutler had been drafted by the Denver Broncos in the first round as the eleventh pick, and as the Broncos' starting quarterback, he'd set a 7–4 record. In fact, the year 2008 had been Cutler's very best on the field, with 4,526 passing yards and 25 touchdowns.

Come 2009, it was incredible that the guy was even available! But lo and behold, rumor had it that the Broncos were actually looking to trade Cutler after his fabulous year, and Cutler apparently wanted out!

True, one could detect a few troubling signs in the candidate's current employment record. Even the press had sniffed out a lot of rancor between Cutler and Broncos management. But reports of rancor didn't seem to bother anyone in Chicago, and they apparently weren't too anxious to investigate deeply or find out how things had gone wrong in Denver after only two seasons.

Instead, the Bears leaped at the opportunity of such a great hire. They offered Cutler $54 million, guaranteed in a seven-year deal. Sometime later, when he seemed to need a little more motivation, they upped him to a $126 million contract. Sure enough, come August 2009, he started as the great hope of the very hungry Bears.

THINGS GO SOUTH

Pretty much from day one, Jay Cutler was a disaster for Chicago. Not because he couldn't throw. He could definitely throw; he could definitely *play the game,* even sometimes win.

But he was absolutely terrible as a *leader,* both on and off the field.

If they had asked around in Denver, the Bears might have discovered that Cutler was a first-class prima donna. An out-of-control diva. In Chicago, he quickly became known as an egomaniac who was "surly and unlikeable," as one sportswriter put it. An "immature" player who showed every passing emotion on his face, yelled at ball boys, scowled at his fellow players, gave the finger to photographers, and threw tantrums when things went wrong. Plenty of times, he was caught cursing out teammates on the field, and several times, he was seen wiping back tears on camera.

Rolling Stone called him "the eternally dour quarterback," and *The Onion* called him "the quarterbitch." Many of his new teammates openly hated him.

In short, Cutler was a man who should never, ever have been given a leadership role in a billion-dollar organization. No matter how hungry that organization might be. By the time the Bears finally got rid of their golden boy—a long and tumultuous eight seasons later—the entire city of Chicago heaved a sigh of relief.

What went wrong? Hey, didn't Cutler have a great resume? Winning stats? How could the Bears have made such a bad decision?

More importantly, how could they change their process to make the right decision about hiring leadership next time around?

QUALITIES MATTER

Unfortunately for both the Broncos and the Bears, great skills and talent—even absolutely, positively proven skills and talents backed up with hard stats—are not enough to go on when you set out to hire a leader.

Because guess what? A leader must have more than skills and talent. They must also have those often-cited but rarely found "leadership qualities." A leader must be the person who is always optimistic. The person who rallies others in the face of adversity. Who doesn't yell and scream. Who brings people together. Who focuses on what people can do instead of what they can't. Who people *want to work with* and want to impress by doing great things.

It's leaders like that who build the futures of organizations. Who create winning teams over the long haul. Not just talented men with good arms.

Leadership qualities cannot be read on a resume. They cannot be seen in sales numbers or organizational growth stats.

And if, like those very hungry Bears, you hire a leader without such qualities, *especially in an age when everything in business depends on exceptional leadership,* the results for your organization are guaranteed to be catastrophic.

MAYBE YOU'VE BEEN HUNGRY, TOO

Perhaps it has sometimes been your job to hunt down a candidate for a leadership role in your company: VP, COO, department head, regional manager, or even CEO.

Like the Bears, you were under a lot of pressure. Everyone saw the glaring vacancy on the org chart, the obvious vacuum at the top, the empty seat at the table. People felt adrift, rudderless. And you were told, "Listen, it's paramount to fill that role ASAP!"

Under that kind of stress, you may have become pretty enamored of a highly decorated resume. You may have read a list of accomplishments with mounting excitement. And when you finally got that person in for an interview, you really *wanted* them to interview well. You were *eager* for them to impress you, and you really wanted to impress *them.*

And guess what? As a result, the interview went great!

In fact, maybe like the Bears, you ended up rushing the process. Not really doing your homework. Not really taking the time to dig into who this person was as a human being. Not finding out whether he or she aligned with the mission of your organization. Not fully investigating their leadership style.

Truth be told, you really had no idea whether this was a person who would stay calm in a storm. Inspire a team. Not go crying in front of TV cameras. But you hired this person anyway, in a hurry, because *who knew who else might be courting them?*

And then, surprise. You found out who they really were.

Maybe even on day one.

WE'VE BEEN THERE, TOO

Both of us—Max and Brian—have been there, done that, and made our own very big mistakes. As entrepreneurs and as long-term recruitment professionals, we've seen plenty of hires go bad. Hires who looked really damn good on paper.

Over the years, we've learned that the world is full of Jay Cutlers.

For example, Brian once recruited a guy—we'll call him Jackson—to backfill Brian's own position at a big company when he got kicked upstairs. Jackson had an incredible resume. He got his MBA from a top-ranked business school. He'd played at high levels in places like Merck and Pfizer, where he'd held impressive positions, and he had assistants for everything. Jackson could use the biggest business words and talk the biggest business theory around.

Plus, the guy had a really nice suit. With French cuffs. And cufflinks.

Brian was super impressed. "I remember thinking, 'How lucky we'd be to get this guy!' And then we did get him. And it was a train wreck."

By the second month, it was obvious to Brian and to everyone else that Jackson wouldn't work out. Why? "Even though we were a casual high-tech company, he showed up in that same damn suit he'd interviewed in, cufflinks and all. He just didn't get us, and it should have been obvious that he would never get us.

"But mostly he just wasn't willing to *do the work*. Jackson only wanted to hold meetings and talk theory all day—just like in his amazing interviews. But when it came down to it, he simply wouldn't pick up a phone and call a client. Or sit down and hash through a real problem on a real project. He couldn't even be bothered to configure his own email account.

"In retrospect," says Brian, "I should have seen the writing on the wall. He came from the wrong kind of environment for us—and yes, the suit should have been a tip-off. We weren't a big company with a bunch of assistants waiting to help him out. All that MBA stuff was impressive but actually irrelevant to our needs on the ground. His big pharma experience sounded great but truly had nothing to do with a small high-tech startup.

"As for me, if I'd done just a little digging to find out more about Jackson as a person, I would have seen he had been operating at too high a bureaucratic level. I would have recognized that we needed someone who offered both high-level strategy *and* some boots-on-the-ground moxie."

ANOTHER TRAIN WRECK

In his previous life as an entrepreneur, Max has been there, too. "I once hired a woman—let's call her Caroline—as my VP of business development. This Caroline apparently had all the right background in market analysis and bringing new ideas into a company. I read her resume back and forth, I examined her previous successes, and she shone in the interviews—but I never really dug into the personality or leadership style of this very important hire.

"Right off, Caroline was a disaster—on two counts that I should have seen coming. She had zero idea of how to work with an operations group on actually delivering a product, new or otherwise. So, in short order, our operations folks hated her for her unrealistic expectations and apparently random demands. How had this worked at her previous positions? I realized I had absolutely no idea.

"Secondly, and even worse, Caroline simply could not keep her personal life out of the office."

Now, everyone has a personal life, and throughout this book, we advocate engaging with people both personally and professionally. But there's a point where it can become a problem. It turned out Caroline had a terrible relationship with her husband. They were headed for divorce, and Child Protective Services had actually been contacted.

"She'd call in 'sick' with emotional issues," remembers Max, "or she'd bring up her family issues at the most inappropriate times. We could see her disintegrate right before our eyes—clothing, everything. She'd show up in an old sweatshirt, hair a mess, because she'd stayed in a hotel after a fight with her husband.

"In short, Caroline had most of the *skills,* but she was a loose cannon as a *person,* and it was ugly when we let her go. Ugly for everyone. The hassle and the lost time created a real setback for our company."

Max didn't quite experience a $100-million-plus setback like the Bears. But it was painfully expensive nonetheless.

LOOKING FOR THE "Y"

We started our executive search company, Y Scouts, because we almost *always* saw people hiring leaders in all the wrong ways, making all the same mistakes we'd made early in our own careers as entrepreneurs and recruiters.

With Y Scouts, we wanted to figure out how to hire leadership with the absolute highest probability of success—making damn sure that our clients never again made a Cutler mistake, a Jackson mistake, or a Caroline mistake, no matter how hungry their teams might be.

This book is a direct outgrowth of the philosophies and best practices we've developed at Y Scouts and represents the fruit of our decades of experience in search, along with the hundreds of leadership outcomes we have witnessed, both good and bad, in companies big and small.

What's with the *Y* in Y Scouts?

That *Y* is rooted in a management theory going back to the 1960s, known as Theory X versus Theory Y. The Theory X version of management assumes that employees are basically lazy and must be motivated with carrots and sticks. That people will do as little as possible in the absence of tight structure and supervision.

In direct contradiction, Theory Y management believes that people *want* to do good work. Theory Y assumes all workers are intrinsically motivated to improve and find meaning in their jobs. Most importantly, Theory Y believes that it's the job of leaders to inspire as much as to manage.

We firmly believe in Theory Y. We firmly believe that *in*

the modern business environment, Theory Y leaders have a far higher chance of success. Maybe the only chance of success.

This book is all about recruiting, vetting, hiring, and enabling Theory Y leaders. This means men and women with, yes, "leadership qualities"—a subject we will discuss in depth to get past the platitudes and BS that often surround that phrase. We will focus on such qualities, because they define Theory Y leaders as much as they define the best and most successful companies operating today.

A DEEPER SYMBOLISM

From the perspective of both leaders and workers, the letter *Y* also has a deeper symbolism. If you look at the letter as an image, and you start from the bottom, you can think of traveling in a straight line until you reach a fork in the road.

In everyone's life, but especially in the lives of the exceptional people who rise to leadership, we all come to this fork in the road. Go one way, and you can continue to simply climb the ladder—the next job up, the grander title, the bigger paycheck. Make the other choice, and you are called upon to blaze your own trail, following your heart and soul to do the kind of work that really matters to you.

And yes, when you get to that fork in your career, you inevitably face the question "Y?"—or rather, "Why?"

We believe that the best leaders take that second road, the road less traveled, and find a company to match their passions, often regardless of the paycheck. We also believe that companies in the present day only truly find their success when they find those perfect matches—leaders inspired by their culture and mission, who are ready to inspire others.

Jackson was no match for Brian's organization. He had no true passion for the work and no ability to inspire others with his passion. Taking that job under Brian meant nothing to Jackson but another "career step." The same proved true for Caroline, and ultimately for Jay Cutler, who clearly had no interest in the Bears as a team.

Making the right choice at the Y fork matters for more than just leaders. In this book, you will also learn how great leaders help everyone else in a company find their road to passionate engagement, too.

MORE ON THEORY X AND THEORY Y

Who dreamed up Theory X and Theory Y? These two basic ideas about how to manage people were first defined by social psychologist Douglas McGregor while working at the MIT Sloan School of Management back in 1957. During the 1960s, McGregor's ideas were much discussed and developed and helped lead to some of the changes we've seen in the industry today.

Theory X is old school and based on military hierarchies. It demands "strict supervision, external rewards, and penalties" for employees. Basically, Theory X is pessimistic about human beings. It assumes that most workers try to avoid responsibilities and care only about themselves. It also assumes that workers are dumber than managers.

Theory Y presents an inherently optimistic view of people and focuses on "job satisfaction and encouraging workers to approach tasks without direct supervision." Theory Y assumes that people really do want to do good work, want to enjoy their labor, and want to improve themselves. Under Theory Y, employees are considered valuable as human beings, not just cogs, and it's believed that they will do best when given increasing autonomy and responsibility.

IMPROVING EVERYONE'S WORK LIFE

For the last couple of decades, the Gallup organization has measured something called "employee engagement," which could be considered a measure of the health of the workforce. According to this measure, roughly seven out of every ten US employees say they are unhappy with their work experience.

Polls are imperfect, but we have no reason to dispute

this staggering statistic. Even if the poll were somewhat inaccurate, we do not believe that a majority of Americans should be spending a majority of their waking hours doing something dissatisfying or even distasteful to them.

Employee engagement polling shows something just as important. It shows that employees believe that the leadership of their companies *could* make those same jobs more satisfying and more rewarding *if those leaders just tried.*

Think about that. The right leaders, with the right attitude, could vastly improve the daily experience of tens of millions of their fellow Americans—and of course, worldwide. The right leaders could change the narrative around work of all kinds so that work becomes more than a means to a paycheck. So that the meaning of one's life can be played out on more than evenings and weekends.

We created Y Scouts to help companies realize that the biggest untapped potential in the business world is not capital. Not strategy. Not market conditions. Not technology.

It's people.

Because people with heart and soul—people who believe in a greater purpose—are the driving force behind the highest performing and most competitive companies today.

Lots of companies have traditionally said, "People are our most important asset." Now they have to mean it.

Why? Because today's most talented workers are coming to their own personal forks in the road, and those best workers will *only* be satisfied by companies and leaders who can articulate purpose, values, and a worthwhile corporate culture.

But how do you find such leaders?

LET'S BE CLEAR: IT AIN'T EASY

Before you get much further in this book, let's get extra-clear about one thing.

As we said in the opening, finding the right Theory Y leaders and matching them to the culture and mission of your company will require a whole lot more of your time and effort than posting jobs and looking at resumes. *A whole hell of a lot more of your time and effort.*

Right now, we're guessing that if you are responsible for hiring leadership in your company—division heads, VPs, COOs, you name it—you are probably going about one of the most important projects you will ever undertake all wrong. Way wrong. We can say that with confidence because just about everyone we meet goes about this all wrong.

Doing it wrong means doing it in a hurry, without involving enough stakeholders, making the right preparations, or completing the required homework.

Doing it wrong means doing it the way it has always been done: postings, resumes, a short series of interviews, and then boom, someone gets hired. Only much later do you realize exactly *who* got hired.

With this book, we want to convince you to hire in a completely new way. We want you to hire like the life of your business depends on it—because it does. In fact, the working title of this book was *Hire Like Your Life Depends on It.*

BUT Y LISTEN TO US?

Both of us, Max and Brian, have decades of leadership recruiting experience at companies large and small. Okay, no resume inflation: between us, at this writing, we have precisely thirty-nine years of experience in recruiting.

So what do our resumes look like?

After Max graduated college in 1998, he worked for Aerotek as a recruiter specializing in telecommunications. "These guys had the hard skills recruiting process down solid, and I learned a lot about vetting resumes and candidates, even if they weren't so hot at scoping out soft skills."

By 2002, he had started his own company, called Job Brokers.

"The name of my first recruiting company seems pretty ironic to me now," says Max. "Executive-level folks don't look for a 'job' anymore, and most think that 'broker' is actually a four-letter word. But in 2002, those words still resonated, and my company grew extremely quickly—by more than 100 percent every year for five-plus years—until we were doing about $40 million a year.

"Job Brokers started in engineering and design but moved into manufacturing, solar engineering, education, and aerospace—and placed literally tens of thousands of people through contract-to-hire and direct hire. For example, we worked with a new utility solar company and helped it grow from $1 million to $80 million a year, recruiting nearly all its leadership and over 500 production workers."

As for Brian, back in 2000, he was a founding member and innovator at one of the first viable online job boards, called Jobing.com. It started just as the web was taking the market away from local newspaper classifieds. "The web offered unlimited space to tell your story as an employer," notes Brian. "And suddenly candidates could very quickly and easily send their resume with one click. It changed everything."

After eleven years at Jobing.com, Brian was wooed away to a position with P.F. Chang's and Pei Wei restaurants as their first-ever director of talent acquisition.

"At P.F. Chang's, I was suddenly a buyer instead of a provider of executive search services. We hired the Spencer Stuarts and the Korn Ferrys of the world to find leaders throughout our organization. But I was totally underwhelmed by their services. These recruiters were nice people, but their visions proved extremely limited, and their restrictions were absurd. We'd say we needed a new chief marketing officer, and they'd say, 'Listen, Brian, here's a list of all the restaurant companies we *can't* recruit from, because we did work for them before, and we have off-limits agreements. Here's the list we *can* recruit from. Which do *you* like best?'

"I'd just stare at these guys. 'You're kidding, right?'

"Never did these staid, cautious firms think of introducing candidates from *outside* the restaurant industry—as if people might have some *new ideas* to offer. They were just moving pieces around on the chessboard of the big, existing chains."

Brian's frustration with the leading executive search firms led him to say to himself, "Wow, if this is the way the biggest and most successful firms are operating, there's definitely an opportunity to carve out a new niche in this space with a company doing it differently and better."

Meanwhile, Max had begun to question the quality of his own success.

"My company was making tons of money, and I was taking home seven figures, but I began to feel that I was not helping my clients in the long run. Not fixing the roots of their problems, only giving them short-term fixes. The focus of our service was contract-to-hire, and we'd provide hundreds of bodies to fill positions—but these people were seen by both our clients and us as interchangeable parts. Our clients were not finding the kind of vision and purpose that they really needed from the people we were placing.

"'Recruiting' was becoming entirely *transactional,* without a greater purpose in helping these companies, or their employees, progress. Our work was just about volume. About hiring lots of people, knowing that many of them would not work out—the perpetual revolving door. By 2011, like Brian, I found myself at that Y fork in the road. I wanted to do more. I wanted to find my own purpose in this industry and do some actual good for my clients."

The two of us, Max and Brian, started talking in 2011. By 2012, Y Scouts was born.

From our very first meetings, we had passionate conversations about Theory X and Theory Y, about the human factors in hiring leadership, and how to get past resumes—whether honest or BS—to understand the real person.

Then we asked ourselves, "How the hell do we match that real person with a corporate culture?"

From our extensive experience, we recognized that making such matches at the leadership level is not easy and that the old methods of recruiting were no longer working. So we set out to entirely rethink methods for locating, recruiting, and vetting people able to lead companies to a superb performance in a rapidly changing world.

From the start, Y Scouts definitely did it differently. By now, we know for sure that we do it better.

WHAT'S THE ROI?

If you still haven't decided whether this book is for you, let's pin down the specific ROI.

What's the potential return on investment for your time? What will you gain by reading on?

You will learn why job postings are pretty much a waste of time when it comes to hiring real leaders and how to get the right person without any postings.

You will learn how resume padding and the tailoring of interview answers to specific job descriptions screw up the hiring process. Then you will learn how to escape those traps by doing the proper homework and reframing the whole process. (Here's a hint: try interviewing somebody without telling them what job you're considering them for. No kidding. See chapter 5.)

You will learn how to understand your company's DNA and how to find a person who authentically aligns with that DNA.

You will learn about the connection between your company's mission, its purpose, and its values and finding a person who can guide your company in that mission, that purpose, and those values, day in and day out.

You will learn that "mission," "purpose," and "values" are not just words printed on posters.

You will learn that skills, talents, credentials, and a candidate's proven experience "doing the job" aren't enough and that you really can identify candidates who actually are "enough."

If we succeed in our own mission, this book will up-level all your hiring and move you toward Theory Y leaders who will focus on developing both themselves and their teams. Leaders who will bring a disposition of relentless learning into your culture and drive results. Leaders who will raise your company's performance to meet the never-ending shifts of a new economy.

But we're not just talking theory here.

In these pages, you will find the practical procedures, tools, and tips we have refined through our experience and pioneered in the executive recruiting industry through Y Scouts.

You will learn the proper steps to take at the beginning of the recruiting process; the things to do before talking to a candidate or even advertising an opening for a job; how to look for the "leadership model" during an interview; how to make a proper offer; and ultimately, how to develop good hiring practices throughout your company.

In short, you will learn the Y Scouts Method.

Your hiring system is broken. Let's go fix it.

PART I

Hiring for a New World

CHAPTER 1

How Hiring Must Change

The way you hired leaders yesterday will not work today.

It's that simple.

The business landscape has changed more radically in the last ten years than in the last one hundred years and will continue to change at an accelerating pace—in ways neither you nor we can predict. AI? VR? Social media? Branding? Corporate transparency? Politics? Religion? Open or closed borders? Insourcing? Outsourcing? Homesourcing? Robotics? The role of rock-star CEOs? Don't blink, or you'll miss the next enormous shift.

In the midst of this tectonic activity, not much has shifted in the way most companies hire. Usually, it still boils down to, "If we post it, they will come."

Job boards replaced newspaper classifieds, but it's basically the same old, same old: (1) post a job description, (2) sit around and wait for responses, (3) interview a few leading applicants, (4) make a choice as quickly as possible, and (5) brush off everyone who didn't make the cut as if they no longer existed.

This process completely ignores the transparency of today's business. It ignores the power of social media. It ignores the new reality that your best candidates, even the ones you dismiss, might also be your best customers or clients. It ignores the necessity of leadership attuned to that kind of change—and it certainly ignores the way people now think about work and search for work.

You have to go looking for exceptional people; they won't come looking for you anymore. And you have to do more than post *jobs*; you have to create an environment where exceptional people will seek you out to find purpose, values, and a culture in which they *want* to work.

Before we break down all the problems with the old system of hiring leaders and explain how to do it right in our new business environment, we need to dive into the deeper reasons the old system became outdated—right along with our old definitions of leadership.

THE PAST IS RAPIDLY BECOMING THE PAST

A few decades ago, phrases like *purpose, values,* and *culture* had little meaning in business.

Our parents got up in the morning, took showers, did the commute, clocked in by eight or nine, and the minute the five o'clock bell rang, they left and came home for dinner. Work was work, and home was home: you were one person in your living room and a very different person in your cubicle. Companies focused on "hours put in" more than "results put out." If you arrived before your boss and left after your boss, you would likely climb the promotional ladder.

Always, our parents knew exactly where they stood in the hierarchy. That's because, since the Industrial Revolution, most companies adopted rigid organizational concepts borrowed from the military and the Catholic Church. You know the drill: an unquestioned controlling power at the top, with power distributed downward along a highly defined chart.

In this model, the people at the top made the most important decisions, the people in the middle made less important decisions, and the people at the bottom made no decisions at all—they simply followed rules. Often, the major criterion for moving up was seniority. As you aged and got more experience, you progressed.

This structure worked pretty darn well for business—up to the point when technology began to create massive transparency, more complex interactions among teams, nonstop innovation, and many more buying options for customers.

As we all know, the people closest to the customer are usually in a better position to make, or at least to influence decisions that directly affect customers. And that means the people closest to the customer began to need some independence and decision-making power of their own. Rapid change began to require more fluid organizational structures, and ad hoc initiatives became a necessity for driving innovation.

To make all that work, people had to actually care about what they were doing—and that's why businesses began experimenting with new, flattened structures, enabling more self-management.

NURSES IN THE NETHERLANDS

Take the Dutch company Buurtzorg, which provides

in-home nursing. The founder of Buurtzorg, Jos de Blok, came from an extremely hierarchal and programmed organization, where nurses were routed around the city to perform brief procedures on new patients all the time.

Patients hated all the new faces, the lack of accountability, and the lack of continuity in care.

De Block created an entirely new kind of self-management model in which "cells" of nurses consisting of ten to twelve people would operate autonomously without a boss. Their goal? Provide personal care with just one or two nurses per patient but support one another as a team.

One study showed that Buurtzorg typically uses only 40 percent of the care hours prescribed by a doctor—saving money for the Dutch state that bankrolls healthcare for its citizens.

By 2014, Buurtzorg had taken 80 percent of the in-home nursing market, with a total staff of 8,000 people managed by just 25 at its headquarters.

The company's purpose? Great nursing. The culture? Independence with professional camaraderie. The values? Exceptional work and mutual support.

Some businesses still operate strictly on the old military models, but those businesses are fast becoming obsolete and irrelevant. A comparison of the Fortune 500 list in 1955 versus 2016 shows that only 12 percent of the biggest companies in America survived on the Fortune 500 list after sixty years of change.

Why did the models of household names become irrelevant? Because they could not leverage their people's talents to accomplish change. Because "hours worked," "work versus life personas," and "seniority-based advancement" are horseshit and always were. Just because you're there doesn't mean you're doing a damn thing. Just because you're home doesn't mean you're not still passionately involved with your work.

The right question has *always* been "What are you able to accomplish?" Not "How many hours did it take to do it?" But more and more, the key question has become "Why are you doing it at all?"

Purpose, values, and *culture* have come to matter as much as "market strategy," top to bottom, in every organization. Indeed, in many industries, purpose, values, and culture have become almost *synonymous* with market strategy. Examples include Southwest Airlines, Harley-Davidson, Apple, REI, and Patagonia: all great examples of companies whose stated public missions attract the right talent and drive long-term, sustainable profit. Companies like these realize that the way they make money will be directly tied to the kind of talent they can attract and the way they recruit.

Importantly, we now see up to five different generations working together in a single company—with different generations operating at all levels of the organization, regardless of seniority, and not just on flexible schedules but often with highly malleable job definitions. These generations, along with their changeable roles, must be bound together by a common thread of DNA if they are to work as a team. Otherwise, sheer chaos will result.

What's the only DNA capable of binding everyone together? *A replicable thread constructed of purpose, values, and culture.*

Are we hammering this home yet?

WHAT YOUNGER WORKERS CARE ABOUT MOST

The younger your team, the more focus you will see on purpose, culture, and values. Studies show that people in their twenties and thirties have generally held more jobs than a boomer has in their entire lifetime. This partly arises from the unstable work landscape of our time, but it's partly because the tolerance level for bullshit among young people has grown extremely low. Too much BS, and they bounce.

Why does BS cause them to bounce? Because both millennials and their younger peers recognize that how you spend your days is how you spend your life. And the more time you spend with people you align with, the more enjoyable your life experience will be. If you spend three-quarters of your adult life at this thing we call work, that time must be meaningful in some way, shape, or form. Otherwise, work is a waste of time.

> *Pro tip: we believe millennials are the first generation brave enough to say what every generation has always wanted—meaningful work.*

ALIGNING THE PERSONAL AND THE PROFESSIONAL

Embracing meaning in work is not just good for people; it's also good for business.

It's both a blessing and a curse to be a member of the human race. But as humans, we cannot help but desire meaning and purpose in our lives. At our cores, we seek to be helpful toward others. For most of us, helpfulness is at the very center of purpose. Business is a great mechanism for being helpful—without a doubt, it's the greatest method ever devised for solving the challenges faced by the billions of people inhabiting the earth.

Thanks to social media, collaborative platforms, and the astounding personal transparency of our times, the alignment between who you are at work and who you are as a person gets closer and closer.

Your working teams cannot avoid seeing the challenges and opportunities faced by the world. Every day, everyone in your company is bombarded by these troubles in the media and on social media. You can no longer ask your employees to avoid this call to purpose and action.

Listening to this call does not make your employees lazy or "entitled." Never make the mistake of labeling talented, creative young people as entitled. These folks are willing to work hard, often harder than their parents. They simply want more than money out of the experience.

> *In order to create and sustain a successful company in today's environment, leaders must offer the purpose, values, and culture necessary to bind a team together. Leaders must also meet an individual's expectation for meaning while offering an authentic alignment with their larger identity as a person.*

We will discuss purpose, values, culture, and personal/

professional alignment in detail throughout this book. For now, here are some quick definitions:

Purpose is the valuable difference in the world a company seeks to achieve. Purpose is the larger reason for the organization's existence, beyond its bottom line.

Values are the behavioral expectations of how a group of people treats one another.

Culture is a catchall term for a set of shared experiences, expectations, and goals within a company. Culture is based on purpose and values.

TURNING THE TITANIC

Finding leaders who can articulate and sustain purpose, values, and culture is not easy. And it's painfully slow and difficult to turn a traditional company to face a new world.

Few companies even recognize the shift in worker expectations. Even fewer try to turn their ships. Most sail merrily along like the Titanic, headed for an iceberg they cannot visualize. These days, you see the wreckage everywhere: Sears, Blockbuster, Toys"R"Us, Kodak, Polaroid, GM, Dalton Books, Tower Records, Compaq, Sun Microsystems.

Unfortunately, even when old-style companies want to

course correct, they rarely know how. Business schools don't often teach the softer side of business. It's still P&L, sales, strategy, and marketing. Business schools have a tough time even *thinking* about purpose, values, and culture because such things are hard to quantify, difficult to measure, and uncomfortable to teach.

This discomfort and difficulty, however, does not change the fact that all the best people out there crave a deep sense of meaning and fulfillment from their work and the impact their organizations create in the world.

They'll find it somewhere, just maybe not at your company.

NEW MANAGEMENT STRUCTURES

As companies try to move toward Theory Y values, they are also seeking new ways to organize. Some of the new DNA structures, like the concept of "holocracy," have proven highly successful, at least in some cases. Certainly, these structures are more responsive to our need for meaning in the workplace.

In a holocracy, authority and responsibility are not rigidly defined in an org chart. Instead, the company organizes around individual groups responsible for specific projects or initiatives, each moving forward somewhat independently. Holocratic teams quickly form and dissolve, with members drawn ad hoc from people of the needed skills—regardless of their formal titles.

For example, a marketing person may be leading a team in a new marketing push. But if somebody from the accounting department is really good at organizing meetings, keeping meeting notes, or collecting market data into a usable form, they may be added to the team in a role completely unrelated to accounting.

In this way, a company can truly draw from everyone's talents, regardless of job descriptions written long before the present need arose. As of this writing, experiments in holocracy are showing huge promise at organizations like the Morning Star Company.

The Morning Star Company runs canning factories for tomatoes, tomato paste, diced tomatoes, etc.—probably the last place you'd expect to hear about innovative management techniques. But here's the company's message about self-management, from its current website:

> The Morning Star Company was built on a foundational philosophy of Self-Management. We envision an organization of self-managing professionals who initiate communication and coordination of their activities with fellow colleagues, customers, suppliers, and fellow industry participants, absent directives from others. For

> colleagues to find joy and excitement utilizing their unique talents and to weave those talents into activities which complement and strengthen fellow colleagues' activities. And for colleagues to take personal responsibility and hold themselves accountable for achieving our Mission.

A lot has been written about the Morning Star Company because these folks literally have no managers. None. They are truly self-managing.

But even companies sticking to old-style management hierarchies have found that the old Theory X mentality of distrusting the judgment of employees has had to be adjusted. In a world where people are working from wherever, at whatever times, and collaborating with great openness on platforms like Slack, managers are pretty much forced to loosen their grips.

RESPONDING TO NEW MODELS

Regardless of the organizational model within your company, effective leaders in today's business culture must lead by being inclusive of everybody. They simply cannot function successfully with a purely top-down mentality. Information travels too quickly, and collaborative interactions now cross too many boundaries.

For example, a brutal organizational model still followed

in some large companies is known as “stack ranking.” Former GM CEO Jack Welch popularized this model back in the 1980s, and many companies, including giants like Microsoft, followed his lead for years.

In stack ranking, managers are required to rate their employees on a bell curve in which only about 10 percent are allowed to be called “top performers.” A similar set number must be ranked as “low performers” *and must be fired each year*. Hence, stack ranking is sometimes called “getting rid of the bottom.”

Few management concepts are worse for employee morale than stack ranking, and over time, such companies began to lose ground. In 2009, about 49 percent of top companies said they used stack ranking. By 2011, only 6 percent still did. Microsoft officially dropped stack ranking, a favorite policy of CEO Steve Ballmer, only in 2013.[1]

Before social media and the like, only bottom performers might feel miserable under such a system. Thanks to rigid hierarchies and information boundaries, fears and anger could be contained. These days, however, collaborative models and technologies ensure that the fear will spread throughout an organization, and no one will feel safe.

---

1 Max Nisen, “Why Stack Ranking Is A Terrible Way To Motivate Employees.” http://www.businessinsider.com/stack-ranking-employees-is-a-bad-idea-2013-11.

Leaders must now take account of the "average experience" of every single person in the company. This may sound obvious, but many still discount whole groups of employees as "not smart enough" to realize what's going on. Wrong.

GENERATIONAL COOPERATION

Earlier, we talked about the challenge of multiple generations working together in ways that break the traditional model of seniority—and the need for a company DNA to hold everyone together. Without at least some "holocratic" notions of management, intergenerational opportunities will also be missed.

Members of the boomer generation are not just looking forward to longer lives; they're also pushing back against the notion of retirement. These people have a lot to contribute, and they want to keep contributing. Nevertheless, in the present environment, an older worker may truly not know more about how to do a specific job than a younger worker.

In the right culture, wisdom can become a two-way street: traditional knowledge and experience from older workers can be paired with new kinds of knowledge and experience from younger workers who have grown up in the new world of technology. Sometimes only these younger workers see how to leverage the new world to get things done.

What org structure for your company will capitalize on the talents and experience of both older and younger workers? What leaders can you hire to envision and sustain such a structure?

THE CHALLENGE OF TRANSPARENCY

If there's one common theme running through this chapter, it's transparency. Today's leaders must recognize that this often-overwhelming transparency operates both internally and externally. When everyone is able to communicate with everyone, simultaneously and in real time through social media, the "employment brand" of a company will inevitably become almost identical to its "customer brand."

There's no avoiding it.

Your head of HR, your head of marketing, and your investor relations person had better get their messaging aligned. If not, people inside and outside the company will reveal the inconsistencies with astounding speed.

Everyone is now a stakeholder in every piece of information, including, of course, customers posting reviews on your website. How does this relate to employees? Check out Glassdoor.com, where employers are rated by employees on leadership, culture, and compensation. Even specific managers get rated.

Because we live in a time when everyone is entitled to a public opinion about everything, your brand becomes the brand of your ambassadors. Those ambassadors are no longer just your marketing team, your salespeople, and your best customers but also your accounting folks, your suppliers, your vendors, and for those who do it well, even your competition.

Will the leaders you hire be able to manage this transparency, even thrive within it?

THE END OF WORK-LIFE BALANCE

One result of all the above has been the end of the old, misguided idea of a "work-life balance," which dominated our discussion of work for decades. This so-called balance assumed that "work" was so grinding and taxing that in order to survive as a human, you needed to escape from work through your "life."

Here at Y Scouts, we don't think there's any such thing as a work-life balance. If you need an escape from your work because your work is a soul-sucking experience, we don't care how much you balance that off on the weekend. We think your life still sucks. If you hate your work, you should find something that doesn't drain your soul, and you should try your damnedest to be the same person at work as you are at home.

Yes, you need a break from work. It's always nice to completely disconnect and spend time with your family. But more and more people today are searching for a way to integrate everything that makes existence meaningful into their "life."

Your whole life should be valuable, on the job and off.

Millennials and their younger peers seem to understand this great truth instinctively. And the best among these generations simply will not work in a place that does not grasp the *requirement* of integrating life and work. These talented younger people demand a workplace where they can feel authentic, be allowed to talk openly, and do their jobs free from the fear of judgment by Theory X standards.

THE VALUE OF SCREW-UPS

Importantly—and crucial to your own success as a company—this freedom includes the freedom to fail, because these generations know that failures are where successes come from. That learning and experimentation are the only true roads to success in our time.

Here, we can't help but retell a story from Kristen Hadeed's terrific book, *Permission to Screw Up*.

Kristen founded a company called Student Maid, where one year she hired a summer intern to help with HR. The intern's job was to input data to payroll, and after Kristen trained the woman, she set her loose.

Now, if there's one thing you don't want to screw up, it's payroll. But on her very first effort with the system, the intern put the dollar amounts into the hours column, and vice versa. As a result, she created an error that overpaid the freelance maids by a total of about $40,000. Kristen only found out when some hugely bonused maid was honest enough to call in about the error.

Kristen could have jumped into the system and fixed the problem herself in a few minutes. She could even have shown the intern how to fix it. But instead, she sat the woman down and said, to paraphrase, "Here's what you did; how are you going to fix it?"

In a matter of hours, the intern figured out all the complicated steps to fix the problem and corrected the payroll. Not only did she learn from her mistake, but she also realized she had the ability to problem-solve, and her value as an employee immediately increased. Kristen says that watching this process was one of her most rewarding moments as a CEO.

Indeed, in some companies, recovery from failures is now celebrated as a natural part of an employee's progress. At WebPT, a company we will discuss more deeply later on, they give out a trophy labeled "Fuck Up/Own Up." When someone makes a mistake, owns up to it, and fixes the issue, they get a trophy to set on their desk for all to admire.

Today's leaders must recognize that they are responsible for the success of not only themselves but all these other people as well. Leaders must be the first in a company, not the last, to understand that we will never again see a clean separation of "person" from "worker."

LET'S COUNT THE WAYS YOU'RE DOING THIS WRONG

How do you find leaders who can handle all the changes in the way people see work and find work? Leaders who can create authenticity, honesty, purpose, values—and a great culture for success?

Not the way you're doing it now.

In fact, let's count the ways you're currently going about this all wrong.

1. YOU'RE *STILL* RELYING ON POSTS AND RESUMES

You are simply not going to find great leaders for any level of your company by posting to job boards, then reading the resumes that happen to roll in. It's pretty much lunacy to think that when you get one hundred replies to a post, you're choosing from the best one hundred people available for your position.

These days, only average candidates base their searches on job boards and job descriptions or rely on their resumes to convey their worth. Exceptional leaders know their value, and they are almost exclusively being recruited by savvy companies on the basis of that value rather than "applying for jobs."

When we interview exceptional candidates—whether CEO, COO, CSO, CIO, VP, division head, or any other key position—we usually ask how they found their last job. It's extremely rare that exceptional people read a post. They were almost *always* referred by somebody they worked with, or they were aggressively recruited, either by the primary company or a search firm.

Pro tip: it should raise a red flag if a candidate has been pushed, rather than pulled, out of most of their positions. Exceptional leaders will be pulled out by new opportunities, not usually asked to depart.

Incredibly, HR departments, boards of directors, and hiring managers of all kinds often do not seem to understand that the game has changed, even though they themselves did not achieve their goals by searching job boards.

2. YOU DON'T REALIZE YOU'VE LOST YOUR LEVERAGE

Of all the flaws in the old system, the biggest may be the assumption that companies still have all the leverage in their relationship with key hires. It's now simply dumb to assume that lots of qualified people are out there, wanting your job, and you just need to pick and choose among them.

The power has shifted to the talented.

Why? Because exceptional leaders know that companies are desperate for new leadership. They are in constant conversation with other leaders in their industry and ever aware of *possibilities* opening up. Never mind postings.

Don't be fooled into thinking that this change in the balance of power has come only in the tech professions. As of this writing, unemployment is low, but you have to understand that *in a rapidly changing environment, the exceptional leaders in every industry will always be in short supply*. Because of the way information now moves, and because of the changing attitudes toward "jobs," exceptional people will, from now until forever, find it easy to both find and leave positions.

3. YOU'RE NOT DEVOTING ENOUGH RESOURCES

Even when the people doing the hiring "get it," they rarely *do* anything about it.

Very few companies work hard enough to compete for exceptional people in the current environment. Exceptions include successful companies like Google, Apple, Facebook, Amazon, Southwest, REI, and Patagonia—not coincidentally, the same companies we often cite for focusing on purpose, values, and culture.

Why do you need to put in so much effort? Because if you want exceptional leaders in the new world, you must put in the effort to stay in touch with them all the time. You must stay connected. You must be ready to catch them at the right moment in your timeline and in theirs—the moment when it makes sense for a move.

To pull that off, you must track five to ten leaders for any specific role over an extended period of time—in other words, always. There's just no other way to do it well.

Instead, if most companies want a new SVP of sales, they still wait for the old one to leave, and then they tell their HR department to rewrite and post a new job description or hire a recruiting company *as a single transactional event.*

Incredibly, after the hire has been completed, the unused resumes are then thrown away, and contact is broken off with the "losers." A couple of years later, the cycle begins again.

4. YOU'RE CREATING A LONG, USELESS JOB DESCRIPTION

As part of the old process, the typical "job description" (JD) has itself become hopelessly outdated.

Let's assume that a company needs a new SVP of sales, reporting to the COO. It's pretty rare for that COO to stop, take a deep breath, and really think about what matters most in the SVP of sales role—either now or into the future.

Instead, the COO will ask HR to dust off an old JD for posting. In an attempt to modernize this JD, HR may go visit LinkedIn, Monster, or CareerBuilder; do a search for "SVP of sales" ads from within their industry; and try to piece together something a bit updated. Rarely does anything get deleted in this process. Instead, the JD gets packed with more and more laundry list items—which mean less and less to everyone involved and look increasingly unappealing to candidates.

A JD may be the first encounter a candidate has with your company. If it's filled with all kinds of biz school babble, exaggerated expectations, and literally dozens of "responsibilities," candidates may think you are simply disorganized and unrealistic.

Left out of these long, off-putting JDs may be the issues that really matter to the company. Why? Because no one asked the people who knew and cared most about those issues.

5. YOU'RE NOT INVOLVING ENOUGH STAKEHOLDERS

Any number of stakeholders *inside or outside* the company may have valuable opinions about what matters most in the SVP of sales role. Like, for example, your salespeople. Or even your customers. Such stakeholders may have an extremely clear idea of what competencies a new SVP should bring to the table or what sort of experiences might get a better result than the person vacating the role.

But no one asked.

Usually, even for the most important leadership roles in a company, only one person plus HR becomes involved in the process. Partly, that's because the process is reactive instead of proactive.

The more stakeholders you collect input from when you define a role, the more your chances of success increase in two ways. One, you will have a more complete and accurate picture of what success looks like in the role. And two, you get more people bought into contributing to what success looks like in that role. Both significantly up your chances of a great hire.

Later in this book, we'll lay out a clear process for gathering stakeholder input.

6. YOU'RE NOT WILLING TO WATCH THE FIRE BURN

In general, important leadership positions are filled too quickly. It's that simple.

The COO hears, "The VP is leaving! The VP is leaving! Get us a new VP fast!" So they rush to HR to put out the fire instead of seeing what opportunities for change the fire itself may represent.

Few are willing to sit and watch a fire burn, even for a little while, staring at it to understand the best way to not just extinguish that fire but also build anew. Even fewer invite others within the organization to sit and look at the fire in order to give their opinions, too.

Practically no one asks outsiders for their opinion, even though, as in most things, the customer may know best.

We'll talk more about job descriptions for leaders later on and how they should come at the end—not the beginning—of an internal process. For now, let's just say, "Keep it short, keep it simple, keep it positive, involve the right stakeholders, and focus on successful outcomes instead of 'responsibilities.'"

7. YOU'RE FIXATING ON YOUR INDUSTRY

The old hiring process makes another outdated assumption. It almost always assumes that the best leaders will come from inside one's own industry, on the theory that hiring from within your industry will minimize the learning curve.

Now, no one would argue that it's a bad idea to focus on hiring from within your industry. But this focus must not become an obsession, and in the new world, it may be a serious detriment. You must at least open your mind to the possibility that leadership skills can be transferred from a completely different realm.

That SVP of sales offers the perfect example. When you've sold a product and led a sales team, it's certainly possible that you can lead sales in another industry. In fact, just about everyone would agree that sales leadership can transcend industry. Nevertheless, in the recruiting companies we left behind, we were almost always told, "Go poach someone from my competitors. Stay within my industry. Otherwise, it's going to be far too hard to learn what we do!"

8. YOU'RE FOCUSED ON THE PAST

There's a saying in the military that "generals always fight the last war." The same can be said of hiring those generals. Whenever a leader leaves a key position, those doing the hiring tend to focus only on the shortcomings of the person leaving: "We have to make sure we fill that gap!"

With that focus, however, you miss a huge opportunity—a golden chance to look toward the future and anticipate the next battle. By examining only the qualities of the *retiring* general, you may never ask, "What qualities do we need now to help lead us into the future?"

It's hard work to define those qualities—work we will do together in the chapters to come. But if you fail to do that work and to recruit leaders with those qualities, you will always be filling gaps instead of inspiring your troops.

9. THE MOST DECORATED SAILOR OFTEN WINS

The old hiring process makes another dangerous assumption. To switch to a somewhat less military analogy, it assumes that the "most decorated sailor" in a current crew will make the best captain to lead the ship.

In other words, the old process assumes that strong skills and long experience within an organization will translate into leadership for that organization.

Too often, this assumption proves terribly wrong. Why? Because the qualities that make a reliable and highly decorated sailor, or "the most successful individual contributor," may not at all be the qualities required of a captain. No matter how well they know the ship.

Worse, by short-circuiting the process in this way and failing to step back and define the leadership qualities needed for a specific role, a strategic opportunity for growth and forward-thinking will have been lost.

10. YOU LOOK FOR A MIRROR IMAGE

Let's close off this summary of "the old, bad way" of hiring with the easiest of all mistakes to make.

We all tend to hire people just like ourselves. We do this

either consciously or unconsciously, but we often do it to the detriment of our companies.

We will talk a great deal about looking for leaders who will be a "cultural fit" for your organization. A good fit is vital, but that does not mean hiring for sameness of background, ethnicity, religion, or business school.

It's all too easy to end up with a company of people who all think alike because they all come from the same cultural assumptions. You fail to get healthy debates. You fail to get meaningful, if sometimes uncomfortable, conversations. You fail to get insight into broader groups of customers.

Groupthink is a clear and present danger to every company. If you're not careful, you end up with a herd. Herds are rightly famous for stampeding over cliffs.

STRIKING THE BALANCE

When you hire leadership, you must lead not with skills but with culture. You must put leadership qualities *ahead* of experience. Because a good leader must have it all. You cannot say, "This candidate has the skills; I'm sure they will learn how to lead." You cannot say, "I'm sure this candidate will adapt to our ways over time."

All of which is not to say you can ignore performance. It's

certainly true that a person can have all the purpose in the world and all the caring in the universe while being unable to make decisions, manage large-scale projects, or create results. The best intentions can still lead to bankruptcy. Now that we have moved away from rigid hierarchies and highly defined roles, leaders are often called upon to strike a difficult balance between performance and purpose, profit, and values.

That only means you need better leaders than ever before. Leaders who can be the ambassadors of both your customer brand and your employment brand. Leaders who drive results, ensure profits, develop people, and foster a culture of relentless learning. Because learning crushes knowing, every time.

CHANGING THE NARRATIVE

As you can see, the goal of this book is to change not just the narrative around hiring leaders but also the narrative around the work they guide.

The good news for employees? Work does not have to be a soul-sucking experience. It can be the most meaningful undertaking of your life—and you can get paid for it, too.

The good news for companies? Humanizing the work

experience now offers the best road to success and profitability.

There's a famous saying from *The Godfather*: "it's not personal; it's only business." Well, business has become personal. The charade—acting like "businesspeople," not showing weakness, and pretending to be invincible—is over.

So is the "business as warfare" narrative, which was openly derived from the hierarchies we adopted from the military.

Here's a new narrative for business: "Life is difficult for human beings. We are all human beings. We see a lot of problems in the world. Let's work together to create and deliver products and services to make this world a better place."

TAKING OFF THE MASK

If you are going to find leaders who embrace that narrative—who will truly fit into your organization; who will get the best performance from their teams; who will create a happy, healthy workplace for everyone; and who can truly steer your company through a new world—you are going to have to find out who they really are.

You are going to have to take off your mask, and you are going to have to get your candidates to take off their masks.

You are going to have to encounter each other not as resumes, but as human beings.

CHAPTER 2

Hiring as Strategy

At first glance, the title of this chapter may seem a bit silly. Do we really need to talk anyone into the idea that hiring is a strategic activity? Who would argue that the right people, especially people in leadership positions, *aren't* crucial to business success?

Every business knows it needs the right people, but it approaches the very subjective and strategic activity of hiring with this often-disastrous attitude: "*Well, we'll see who we can find with the right qualifications, and if they don't perform, we'll look again.*"

That's hardly strategic thinking. It's more like a misapplication of the scientific method: *keep trying experiments, adjust the conditions, and try again.* Hiring managers too often assume that if they have a scientifically designed org chart, a scientifically constructed JD, a scientifically ordered business process, and a scientifically aligned resume, then, presto—they can plug "any qualified person" into the job.

It's no wonder they focus more on the org chart, the JD, the process, and the resume than anything so abstract as leadership qualities.

A LITTLE HISTORY

As we noted in the last chapter, the "plug someone in" assumption can be traced back to the earliest days of belching smokestacks.

When the Industrial Revolution kicked off in England, early 1800s, the new captains of industry didn't really have a model for how to organize crowds of laborers, so they looked to organizations that had dealt with the problem before: the military and the church. Their assumption? Workers, like soldiers, were dumb and dumber, easily switched out at will by higher-ups.

Just like the machines they serviced, early industrial workers were literally considered interchangeable cogs, regardless of their skills or background. And in the early days of low-skilled labor and all-powerful owners, that model worked pretty well. Indeed, the first smokestacks belched spectacularly in a total command-and-control environment.

ENTER SCIENCE

But right after the turn of the twentieth century, someone stepped back to find a more scientific approach. That someone was a mechanical engineer and factory manager named Frederick Taylor, who was certain he could get more out of his workers.

Taylor's mantra will sound familiar: *efficiency and effectiveness*. Part of what came to be known as Taylorism was an attempt to match the skills of a particular individual to a particular job. It seems like pure common sense now, but in the 1910s to 1920s, it was a major innovation to say, "Hey, why don't we actually have guys who can lift one hundred pounds put on the jobs that require the heaviest lifting?"

Taylor's incredibly influential 1911 opus, *The Principles of Scientific Management*, proposed increasing productivity with four key principles:

1. Stop working by rule of thumb and use the scientific method to determine the most efficient way to perform a specific task.
2. Stop assigning workers randomly. Instead, match

workers to jobs based on capability and motivation; then train them to work at maximum efficiency.

3. Stop assuming people will do anything right; monitor worker performance and provide instruction and supervision to ensure efficiency.
4. Stop having managers do actual work; instead, let them spend their time planning and training workers.

Result: another leap forward. Indeed, some credit Taylor with the surge of affluence that crisscrossed the developed world during the twentieth century. His four key principles pretty much still rule our working lives.

Just one piece had to be added to make Taylorism complete.

BUREAUCRACY ADDED TO THE MIX

The next scientist to move the ball was the famous German sociologist Max Weber. Weber focused on bureaucratic structures: dividing orgs into increasingly complex hierarchies with clear lines of authority and control. It was an even deeper dive into work specialization, with a focus on rules and regulations intended to *remove the personality factor of managers, too.*

We emphasized that phrase for a reason. Removing personality from the management equation is *the* guiding principle that drives most hiring that we encounter. It's the "scientific" goal of 90 percent of the org charts and JDs we see.

As science took over management theory, both workers and managers found it harder and harder to be seen as anything but a quantifiable means to an end. And thanks to Weber, eventually even corporate leaders came to be viewed as boxes on an org chart.

Did it work? You bet. Yet new scales of industry were achieved.

Still, all this scientific management did begin to show some negative side effects, even beyond low levels of human happiness. By doing away with personality-based decision-making and charismatic leadership, creativity was sacrificed.

Creativity is more than just a "nice to have."

A bureaucratic leadership model revolves around obeying rules and doing what you are told. In such a system, most workers, managers, and even leadership have no incentive to think outside their particular boxes. Hence, their ability to adapt to change and new challenges at every level of the business grows severely limited.

Sure enough, when the world started changing at increasing speeds, people began to see that the most boxlike organizations began losing ground.

Take the great railroad companies that once dominated America. All their effort went into creating huge organizations that kept their trains running on time. As the world changed, however, their extreme focus on Taylorism and bureaucratic Weberism made it impossible for them to step back and ask the question, "What business are we in?" No one was able to say, "Maybe our business isn't trains; maybe it's transportation...so maybe we need to think outside the boxcar."

A LIGHT IN THE 1940S

Finally, even scientists started rethinking management science. Elton Mayo, a Harvard professor, introduced what came to be known as human relations management in the 1940s. Mayo argued that both Taylor's and Weber's structured approaches were actually less important than emotional factors in determining productivity. Following these new theories, managers were encouraged to consult workers about change, take note of their views, and show actual concern for their physical and mental health.

In Mayo's model, pressure toward efficiency and effectiveness came from the social group rather than the chain of command. Work performed, argued Mayo, had to satisfy the personal subjective social needs of the individual as well as the company's requirements. And this was good for everybody.

Indeed, for a few years, people actually toyed with the notion that consideration for the individual could help business. Today's talk about "team building" can be traced straight back to Mayo.

SCIENCE RETURNS WITH A VENGEANCE

Come the late 1970s and early 1980s, however, "scientific" methods roared back like a freight train. A new class of operations management specialists arose, right along with the advent of computerized management information systems. Perhaps inevitably, given digitization, we entered a time totally focused on quantifiable data and workflow depersonalization.

New and powerful theories like Lean and Six Sigma arose out of Japanese management models and focused on daily, incremental improvement. "Nonstop optimization" became the latest variant on Taylor's efficiency mantra. In many fields, but especially technology, nonstop optimization grew into a kind of religion.

Digitization moved the goalposts again. When all efficiency could be digitally monitored, everyone began to believe all efficiency could be scientifically improved, all the time—regardless of the personalities or happiness of the people being improved.

Did efficiency increase? You bet.

Even when it occasionally led straight to failure and bankruptcy.

THE PROBLEM WITH INCREMENTAL IMPROVEMENT

Over the last few decades, we have come to understand that the biggest problem with a scientific approach to management is exactly the same thing that creates its success: *incremental thinking.*

When an organization focuses only on impersonal, incremental, scientific improvement, it can easily miss the big picture. It can easily lose the hearts and minds of its customers, along with its employees. And it can entirely miss the forest for the trees.

Who is responsible for these failures? Leaders trapped in org boxes and following proven, scientific methods of incremental improvement.

Take BlackBerry. Those guys really did create the smartphone, and for a brief shining moment, they totally owned the corporate smartphone market. But all along, they thought that a tactile keyboard (actual push buttons for numbers and letters) and a closed, secure corporate network were absolutely essential to their customers. As a result, they completely ignored the rise of touchscreens and of standard telecom providers invading the market. They were sure that touchscreens were a flash in the pan, so they went right on incrementally improving those tactile keyboards—until it was too late.

Take the Sony Walkman. Sony pioneered portable music on tapes and then discs, and even had an early MP3 player—but nobody listens to MP3 files on a Sony anymore. Why? Because Sony's bureaucratic leadership just went on scientifically and incrementally improving its products while Apple busted the market open with the iPod and later the iPhone.

Kodak was actually one of the pioneers of the digital camera, but the film business was such a cash cow that it was hard for the greedy, hardheaded leadership of Kodak to let go of film—despite the digital wonders their engineers were coming up with. Kodak had all the technology in the world, all the money, and all the R&D, and everyone *outside the company* could see that the world was moving to digital only.

Surely someone must have stood up at some Kodak board

meeting and said, "Let's face it, guys, the era of film is just completely coming to an end." Then again, maybe no one ever stood up, because Kodak was unwilling to go look for the kind of people who would say something like that.

The takeaway? Kodak's leadership could not escape "continuous optimization," the incremental thinking that ensured that after decades of steady improvements in film, they simply could not stop. For far too long, Kodak leadership tried to straddle both worlds. Right up until the new world left them behind.

It's not just technology companies that make this mistake. Take retail giants like Sears. Take every major newspaper. All were stuck taking incremental steps when great leaps were needed.

It's people who make great leaps, not scientific systems.

It's also people who most often cause disasters, not failures of science or process.

There were plenty of financial regulations and monitoring systems in place before the financial meltdown of 2008. Human greed and excessive risk-taking caused the crash. Right before the 1986 *Challenger* explosion, engineers warned NASA not to launch under the current conditions, but their advice was ignored by management.

The fatal flaw in the automobile air bags made by Takata was known to both Takata and Honda, years before they finally took action in 2014.

These are all tales of bad leadership, not poor optimization.

PENDULUM SWINGING?

Is the pendulum now swinging away from "scientific management" toward respect for visionary leadership, individual judgment, and a corresponding concern for the individual in the workplace? All the evidence points to "yes."

Why? *Because nothing that Taylor or Weber or Lean Six Sigma proposed would have done anything to help BlackBerry, Kodak, Sony, the major newspapers, or the major retailers of the world.*

Thanks to the desperate need for flexibility in every kind of business, the humanity of both leaders and workers has begun to matter more than ever before. Indeed, the modern technology industry is all about its leaders, not about the technology. It's about Steve Jobs, Bill Gates, Jeff Bezos, Mark Zuckerberg, and Susan Wojcicki. Outside of tech, it's about people like Jerry Stritzke at REI and Rose Marcario at Patagonia. It's about who is making the decisions.

> *The most important decisions that businesspeople make are not what decisions, but who decisions.*
>
> —JIM COLLINS, AUTHOR OF *GOOD TO GREAT*

Nothing is absolute, and we don't really mean to disparage the value of Lean Six Sigma and similar systems, which can be crucial to designing workflows and ensuring quality. But anyone in a leadership position in today's world must recognize the limits of their incremental systems of efficiency. Indeed, in a world where anyone can copy your systems and even your product within days, *only* your people can offer you a real competitive advantage.

Got that? Never mind the tired line, "Our people are our best asset." *Your people are your only sustainable competitive advantage.*

The secret to good management in the present world is a blended approach, in which you recognize the many factors leading to performance, including both systems and personalities. But you must tilt toward Mayo and Theory Y management if you are going to get the creativity and drive you desperately require.

You need to hire people with the necessary skillsets. But here's the tagline to the above statements: *if you want the best people, and you want the best from those people, you can no longer ask them to sacrifice their own personal needs.* In fact, you must meet their social, physical, mental, and spiritual needs at a level never seen before.

CHARISMA MUST BE PAIRED WITH CULTURE

Before you approach *hiring as a strategy,* however, you must set aside your own scientific management theories and begin by understanding who you are as a business, what you stand for as a business, and what you are trying to achieve in the world. Why? Because that mission must align with the leader you wish to hire.

When that alignment occurs, it's a beautiful thing. And such alignment offers a far more certain road to success than scientifically constructed org charts.

When the alignment is off, it can and will lead to disaster.

Later in this chapter, we will begin to lay out the concrete steps of the Y Scouts Method to ensure alignment, but for now, let's just talk common sense. In the introduction, we told you about some massive misalignments. Let's look at two more to set the stage.

JCPENNEY MISMATCH

In 2011, JCPenney was struggling to compete in the era of eBay, Amazon, Costco, and Walmart. It didn't want to suffer the same sad fate as Montgomery Ward and the other old-style retailers that once dominated the lower price point on reasonable-quality goods.

Like everyone, the JCPenney board of directors watched the miraculous resurgence of Apple with awe and wanted that kind of magic, too. So they recruited Ron Johnson, the Apple retail exec largely responsible for the Apple Store phenomenon as their new CEO. He'd be their new-economy wizard, waving his wand to save them from extinction.

Johnson's mission was certainly not for the faint of heart. It's not easy to resurrect a dinosaur. And no doubt, Johnson is a brilliant man. But he was totally the wrong wizard for the job.

For starters, Johnson's experience and approach at Apple totally did not translate to a discount retailer. Apple is a premium brand with unbelievable excitement and innovation attached to its name. Its mission in the world is completely different from that of JCPenney. Even its values. The resulting crater should have been obvious to anyone who believes in cultural alignment.

In early 2012, Johnson announced a major overhaul of the JCPenney pricing strategy, with what he called "New Fair and Square Everyday Low Pricing." In other words, fixed prices, no sales, no coupons—just like at Apple stores.

But JCPenney shoppers are really *into* coupons and sales. They are looking for *deals*. No coupons? No sales? The shoppers just stopped coming.

Did Johnson test out his pricing overhaul with focus groups of customers and the like? Nope. He came from the Steve Jobs school, which assumed your customers don't know what they want until you give it to them.

True of iPads. Not true of mattress pads.

Would a more scientific org chart have prevented Johnson's failure? A longer or more clearly written job description? A study of Taylor or Weber?

Uh, no.

SALES CULTURE MISFIRE

Cultural mismatches in new hires can screw your entire business, even below the level of CEO. Here's another unhappy example from a company of our acquaintance.

This company provides large-scale services to the high-tech industry. As a services company, it has a true "servant" mission in the world—and yes, that implies a certain relationship with its clientele, along with a set of values that includes *honoring the processes of its clients.*

If the company had taken time to write down its mission and values, as we prescribe in the Y Scouts Method, it might have actually realized how important that particular value was when it came to hiring leaders.

The CEO wanted a new VP of sales. He also desperately wanted to move his company up to "strategic" and "equal partner" relationships with his clients. Of course, his clients were huge entities like Microsoft, IBM, and Oracle.

When he went looking for a new VP of sales, the CEO decided he wanted a "player" who had cut strategic deals with A-list tech companies. So he hired a guy from a tech giant who had been supplying hundreds of millions of dollars of server equipment to folks like Amazon, in what really were partnership relationships.

We'll call this new hire Fred. Fred was from the industry. He knew how to play at a high level. He'd made truckloads of money for his last company. What could go wrong?

Fred was introduced to key clients at an outdoor party with tiki torches and a marimba band, sponsored by the company during a conference. The party had a lot of booze, and one key client was IBM.

Come about 10:00 p.m., the party's going well, and the new VP of sales is seated at a table with the key IBM contact and his own account rep. Everyone's laughing about something. Fred sees his moment, leans back, and says, "So guys, let's make sure we get something out of this night. We're really looking to expand this relationship into a true partnership here. Make us your exclusive supplier, and we'll drop our pricing by 10 percent."

The account rep nearly spits out his drink. IBM does not, of course, work that way, especially with mere suppliers. No decisions are made at parties, with or without tiki torches. Major decisions require months of preparation, five or six PowerPoint presentations, consensus among stakeholders, the works.

The IBM guy goes instantly cold. He says politely, but clearly laying out the boundaries of their traditional relationship, "Feel free to send me an email next week." And that was that. Indeed, the entire IBM account went downhill after that night and was eventually lost completely—as the company had clearly misunderstood IBM's own values.

Although the new VP lasted another year, he never did conclude any "strategic partnerships."

LEADERS FOCUS ON HIRING LEADERS

Let's look at a couple of subthemes that should be emerging from the stories we've told so far.

The first is that a true leader sees him- or herself not as a *player,* with that word's implied independence, but as a *servant* to the values and mission of the company and its clients. Second, a true leader will hire other leaders with that attitude at every level.

We like to call good leaders "conscious leaders." That means they are conscious of their companies' values and missions, as well as practicing a "conscious capitalism" that includes concern for not just one's own employees but also the world at large.

And yes, they are also conscious of performance. And profits. We'll get to that, too.

EVERY HIRE IS A MILLION-DOLLAR HIRE...

The new sales VP mentioned above lost an account worth well over a million dollars a year to his company. Over the course of his abysmal tenure, he probably lost much more, mostly in missed opportunities that will never be known.

We know one CEO who concluded that *every* hire—at every level—is a $1 million transaction for his company.

Right down to the front line. According to some studies, the average hiring mistake costs fifteen times the employee's base salary in losses to the company. For starters, you have plenty of direct costs to the hiring process, and then that wrong person can do plenty of direct and indirect damage, with repercussions for years. That includes negative impacts on morale and culture at the company.

Easily a million-dollar transaction, every single time.

...AND YOU DON'T DELEGATE MILLION-DOLLAR DEALS

Paul Polman was the CEO of Unilever until very recently—a $60 billion multinational with dozens of brands, including Dove and Gillette. As you might imagine, he's a pretty busy guy. Yet Polman walks the talk when he says, "Our people are our most important asset."

This conscious CEO travels the world visiting different Unilever offices. At every one of these offices, he always makes time to sit in on new hire interviews. It might be just an entry-level role, but Polman truly believes that who Unilever lets in the door is *always* a strategic decision. In order for him to best guide the company, he needs to understand what candidates are talking about, regardless of role, country, and brand.

Most importantly, he demonstrates to all his leaders that they, too, must make time to recruit properly.

Most CEOs, presidents, or other leaders try their damnedest to delegate hiring. They say, "That's HR's responsibility, or the recruiter's; I just don't have the time." Although these other people certainly have a shared responsibility, such leaders are making one of the biggest and most common mistakes out there.

If you try to totally delegate recruiting, realize that you are abdicating truly strategic decisions. You are setting a terrible example. You are blinding yourself to your company's own processes. And just as important, you are failing to stay informed about what's happening in the marketplace.

Look in the mirror. Aren't you also a leader who likes to say, "People are our most important asset"?

Suppose you actually meant those words? How would you act?

ENTER THE Y SCOUTS METHOD

Okay, so now maybe you get it.

Now maybe you realize that you've been doing this all

wrong without even knowing it. You've been making every one of those mistakes we listed at the end of chapter 1. You've been way too hung up on Weber-like org charts, Taylorian effectiveness, and Japanese "nonstop optimization" when you should have been thinking "great people." Worst of all, you've been putting recruiting way down on your priority list and not really thinking of hiring as a strategy.

Fortunately, we know a better way. It's been perfected over decades of experience, and we have used it effectively to amp up the performance at hundreds of high-growth companies.

The Y Scouts Method is not science—but as we have seen, science does not provide the answers to this particular problem. Still, the Y Scouts Method offers a clear process, and it's even based on a nifty mathematical formula:

> *Fanatical Preparation + Radical Alignment = Best Possible Outcome*

If you find that formula daunting, we've done our job. In fact, a corollary to this vital formula is the following:

> *Great recruiting is fucking difficult.*

You have to go at recruiting intentionally and methodically. The devil really is in the details, and you cannot skip any of the steps we are about to give you, or you will never achieve that holy grail, the Best Possible Outcome. You will just keep getting inferior results in your company as a whole, usually without even realizing why.

Maybe you'll even end up like BlackBerry or Kodak.

THUMBNAIL OF THE Y PROCESS

Here's a sketch of the recruiting process we will explore over the next three chapters. It is designed to prevent the mistakes we have seen occur again and again at hundreds of companies.

As you can see from the mathematical formula above, the Y Scouts Method for strategic recruiting cannot offer a guarantee of success: we're talking people, not machines. But we absolutely and personally believe there's no better way for conscious leaders to find and hire other conscious leaders. No better way to recruit people who will help you build a happy, successful enterprise.

As you will see in the below steps, we start with fanatical preparation. Then we seek radical alignment. Part of the fanatical preparation is some true, serious, and genuine soul-searching about purpose and values, *because without defining and understanding your purpose and values, you will never, ever achieve alignment. Not for new hires, and not for your existing folks.*

We owe a huge debt of gratitude for development of our thinking to Ann Rhoades, founder/CEO of People Ink, former chief people officer of Southwest Airlines, and author of *Built on Values.* Ann is on the board of Y Scouts, and we particularly recommend her book for a deeper dive on the values discussion than we can provide here.

We've walked through the below process hundreds of times. Even if you don't have the resources to pull off every step of this process, you can still benefit from the basic philosophy behind it. Even implementing a couple of these changes into your hiring process can yield results that transform your hiring forever.

Here's a 30,000-foot view of the Y Scouts Method:

1. **Start with your own DNA.** Understand and then write down your company's true purpose and values. Add key features of the company culture. This is, of course, a reusable document, which must be updated from time to time. In chapter 3, you will find a DNA survey to help with all that, along with some stellar examples of values statements known as Values Blueprints. Your goal in this exercise? Before you look for

alignment, understand what you want your candidates to align *with*.

2. **Throw out any old job descriptions.** Just trash them. Then involve multiple stakeholders and seek their input about the role. Ask questions to understand the success outcomes that matter most to the people closest to, and most knowledgeable about, the role.
3. **Create an Opportunity Profile.** Again, ditch the traditional job description. An Opportunity Profile should highlight the success outcomes the role is intended to deliver and also highlight the purpose, values, and story of the company. And for goodness' sake, don't share your laundry list of skills/qualifications/experiences; why give candidates the answers to the test?
4. **Create an Ideal Candidate Profile,** again involving your stakeholders. This internal-only document will highlight the purpose-alignment, values-alignment, and career-based evidence and proof points you believe will lead to a successful hire.
5. **Develop a search strategy.** Relying on job postings is not a strategy. Think about where the ideal candidate is right now. Where are they working? In what type of company will you find them? What other industries offer a high degree of experiential transferability?
6. **Conduct informal pre-interviews,** *which do not reveal the actual job title.* We'll show you why and how in chapter 5. Your goal? Get past the masks candidates tend to wear for interviews.

7. **Architect a formal and specific Interview Guide.** Then execute it wisely to avoid the usual interview traps. We will give you examples.
8. **Involve multiple stakeholders in the decision.** Then craft a valid offer. We'll discuss some rules of thumb.
9. **Along the way, don't piss anybody off, even the rejected candidates.** Every industry is now a small village where everybody talks to each other.
10. **Design a beautiful and friendly onboarding process** for your new hire. Because yes, the first few months are crucial to long-term success.

Now let's get to those devilish details.

CHAPTER 3

Start with Values...

Unless you understand your company, you cannot understand what to look for in leaders who will align with your company. It's that simple.

Just like human DNA, company DNA is composed of building blocks. As described in chapter 1, this replicable thread of company DNA is constructed of the following:

1. **Values**
2. **Purpose**
3. **Culture**

Remember that even though these concepts are interrelated, they are not at all the same thing. Neither are they BS, fluff, nor mere posters in lobbies. Your company DNA is the glue, the thread, and the binding that holds your company together. It's that leather strap that keeps the dogs on the sled team in alignment as they drag the sled up the hill. Good DNA demands autonomy for both the individual *and* responsibility to the group, all at the same time.

Let's start by separating these three components of your company DNA.

1. **Values** are the minimally accepted set of behaviors that an organization will tolerate. Values are the way you treat people both inside and outside the organization. They're the common set of principles and beliefs that guide your everyday interactions with everyone you come in contact with. As we will see, values have been placed at number one for a reason.
2. **Purpose** is the reason your company exists. It's *the* guiding light in an otherwise volatile, uncertain, complex, and ambiguous world. Profitability and growth are crucial, yet neither is a strong enough reason for a company's existence.
3. **Culture** is shorthand for the complex set of behaviors that are unique to your environment. Culture is *the way people act in your company* or, as Max likes to put it, *the way shit gets done around here.* A good culture is the clear manifestation of your values and your purpose. People who have demonstrated the kind of behaviors that fit your culture and promote your values are the people you want to hire.

In this and the following chapters we want to teach you how to understand the DNA of your company—or maybe finally define it.

Then we want to show how to turn your values, purpose, and culture into words you can use in your search process and in your interview questions. You may even start to think about how to recognize and reward employees on the basis of values, purpose, and culture.

VALUES: NUMBER ONE FOR A REASON

Without values, both purpose and culture will go south. Indeed, *true company values will become the genesis of both purpose and culture.* That makes the development of values the number one job in understanding your company DNA.

Values are a team sport. Why? Because humans imitate one another in groups and take their cues from both their leaders and their coworkers. In a company with good values, you talk about values. You demonstrate them. You revisit them on a quarterly basis in an ongoing conversation within the company. Most importantly, everyone in the company holds one another accountable to the company values.

WebPT is a fast-growing technology firm offering a

SaaS platform for physical therapists to track their work. When WebPT suddenly leaped from about thirty to sixty employees, it started seeing randomization of its values. People were bringing in habits from many environments, and leadership could see that everyone had lost clarity on how they were supposed to behave.

So WebPT brought its company together for about half a day and did some whiteboarding. They asked themselves questions like, "How do we want to treat each other? How do we want to view each other? How do we want our customers to view us? Our families? What type of company do you want to work for? What kind of work environment do you want to be part of?"

Importantly, this exercise was not merely a top-down, command-and-control effort. It truly involved everyone in the company, with the result being a cohesive social contract among the entire team.

When it was done, WebPT distilled the consensus of nearly four hundred words down to a set of five core values (then added three later on), phrased in a delightfully positive way. You can see them in the sidebar. It started with its company purpose, which was "We believe in empowering the rehab therapy community to achieve greatness in practice." Look closely, and you can also see how these values work to create a *company culture.*

WEBPT VALUES

1. **Service: Create Raving Fans**

We all have different roles to fill, but we're united behind a singular mission: empowering our Members to achieve greatness in therapy practice.

2. **Work Ethic: Be Rock Solid**

We definitely value hard work. More than that, though, we value smart work—work that is innovative, creative, and brilliant.

3. **Accountability: F-Up; Own-Up**

We're humans, not robots—which means mistakes are bound to happen. What will not happen is passing bucks, pointing fingers, or covering our you-know-whats.

4. **Community Outreach: Give Back**

We know how fortunate we are to be in the position to give back, and that's why we make it a point to pay it forward.

5. **Attitude: Possess True Grit**

Even when things don't go according to plan, we maintain the passion, determination, and can-do attitude necessary to right the ship and get things back on course.

6. **Resource Efficiency: Do *Más* with *Menos***

WebPT started lean—with three employees in the back room of a coffee shop—and we never want to lose touch with our bootstrapped roots.

7. **Personality: Be Minty**

We're all about spirit, spunk, and collaboration—and of course, fresh breath never hurts. That kind of energy is contagious, and

Members appreciate our service-with-a-smile approach.

8. **Health and Wellness: Live Better**

Rehab therapy is all about improving quality of life, and so are we. That's why we encourage our employees to make healthy choices for their minds, bodies, and souls.

We also love flip-flops, food trucks, and Nerf guns.

When WebPT goes to hire anyone, leader or not, it keeps this set of values front and center in the process. Got the skills? Great. Now, how have you demonstrated these eight values in the past?

Another thing we love about the WebPT values is that they are not at all generic. These values were formed from the company's specific environment and unique purpose in the world.

Here at Y Scouts, we have an even simpler list of values—and it, too, arises directly out of our particular work and purpose. We talk about these values all the time, and we really do call each other out when one of us has gone off the rails.

We start with "relentless growth," because we firmly believe that being a relentless learner is the most critical value for us and the work we do. We have to approach every search client with a fresh lens to discover its authentic company DNA, and we have to stay open if we want to see the authentic personalities of leadership candidates.

Y SCOUTS VALUES

1. **Relentless growth**
2. **Measure what matters**
3. **Finish what you start**
4. **Pause to appreciate**
5. **Have each other's back**

Ann Rhoades worked at both JetBlue and Southwest—two airlines that disrupted the airline industry with their focus on customer satisfaction. She likes to say it was easy to disrupt the airline space because, to paraphrase, "Everyone else treated their customers like crap, and we just decided we were going to treat our customers like humans."

It worked.

She especially points out JetBlue, which developed a Values Blueprint with her help, directly out of the company's stated purpose: "To Bring Humanity Back to Air Travel." She called it a Values Blueprint rather than a mere list, and it is a great term. Blueprint really conveys the way everything should always be built on a set of values.

WHEN VALUES GO BAD, COMPANIES GO BAD

Every company has a set of values, whether it knows it or not. Sometimes those values suck—and it's not hard to find examples.

Take the inescapable case of Enron. Before its collapse after a staggering accounting scandal in 2001, Enron had about 20,000 employees and did more than $100 billion in annual revenues. It owned or brokered electricity, natural gas, and other vital resources. What brought Enron down? Bad values that led to a distorted purpose and a sick company culture.

Enron prided itself on hiring the best and the brightest. Everyone had pedigrees from Ivy League schools and often came out of the big consulting firms. The company was famous for recruiting the top 1 percent of everyone available and paying huge sums.

This hiring policy made the atmosphere within Enron incredibly competitive. Little by little, although the official list of company values included the word "integrity," the real number one value became "win."

HOW YOU DON'T HIRE IS AS IMPORTANT AS HOW YOU HIRE

Most companies treat the candidates they reject like garbage. Often, they don't even tell them they didn't get the job but rather just stop returning calls and emails.

Thanks to the new transparency we all see on the internet, along with the complete brand experience people now encounter, it matters more than ever how you treat the candidates you don't select or hire. Everyone who encounters your organization influences your brand. And everyone you encounter may be able to help or harm you in the future.

The company Zappos finds itself inundated with applicants every time it advertises an opening. But Zappos has recognized that how it gracefully declines the 90-some percent of failed applicants matters tremendously. Plenty of these people may be customers of Zappos, now or in the future. But if those people apply and are treated like crap, if they never hear back, or they find the company rude, that negative experience will continue to resonate.

Just as importantly, you have to remember that hiring is not a short-term goal; it's a long-term strategy. The best companies are always on the lookout for the best people. That means anyone could bring you a great hire later on, or they could become a great hire themselves in a few years.

A highly qualified high-tech marketing exec we know was courted by a cloud services company—until they discovered he didn't know one of the software packages that appeared around line eighteen on a long job description. After several interviews, the marketing VP said to this candidate, "Why are you wasting my time if you don't know this package? We're done here."

This candidate told us, "Doesn't this idiot know that I'm still going to be in his industry the next day? That I can recommend or not recommend his product to others? That I might have known someone just right for his job? All he had to do was be pleasant, thank me for my time, and express some regret about the long JD, and he would not have made an enemy for himself and his company!"

As search professionals, we deeply understand this truth and wish all our clients did, too. We are also always looking to the future. Plenty of times, we will interview a super-talented individual who just isn't quite ready for the job...yet. Treat them well, and a couple of years later, when they are ready, they will call again, just when they're needed most.

Enron's primary implied corporate value led to gambling with both money and ethics, and we suppose the company's implied purpose could be stated as "score vast sums by any means possible." Over time, the Enron company culture devolved to one of unlimited risk. It became common and accepted to lie to governments. Lie to shareholders. Lie to customers. Artificially manipulate prices.

All those bright people took the cultural example set by leadership to heart, with an inevitable result—it ultimately led to their downfall.

PURPOSE: ACTUALLY IMPORTANT TO SUCCESS

Earlier we said that exceptional candidates today, particularly younger candidates, are looking for more than money. Even for more than a set of positive company values.

They are looking for purpose in their work.

Not so long ago, it sounded rather trite and silly to say that a company had a greater purpose in the world than to earn money for its shareholders. Even stating a goal of providing an honest living and a humane work environment to employees seemed, well, not sufficiently *capitalist.*

But here at Y Scouts, we position ourselves firmly in the growing movement called *Conscious Capitalism.* It's a way of thinking about business that better reflects where we are in the human journey, the state of our world, and the innate potential of business to make a positive impact. In our day, it also helps lead to success.

Conscious Capitalism offers four basic tenets to business:[2]

1. **Higher Purpose**

   In the words of University of Virginia Darden School of Business professor and Conscious Capitalism, Inc., trustee R. Edward Freeman, "We need red blood cells to live (the same way a business needs profits to live), but the purpose of life is more than to make red blood cells (the same way the purpose of business is more than simply to generate profits)."

---

2 Conscious Capitalism, http://consciouscapitalism.org. Accessed online, January 2019.

Although making money is essential for the vitality and sustainability of a business, it is not the only or even the most important reason a business exists. Conscious businesses focus on their purpose beyond profit.

We all need meaning and purpose in our lives. It is one of the things that separates us from other animals. Purpose activates us and motivates us. It moves us to get up in the morning, sustains us when times get tough, and serves as a guiding star when we stray off course. Conscious businesses provide us with this sense of meaning and purpose.

By focusing on its deeper purpose, a conscious business inspires, engages, and energizes its stakeholders. Employees, customers, and others trust and even love companies that have an inspiring purpose.

2. Stakeholder Orientation

Pioneering naturalist John Muir observed that "When you tug at a single thing in nature, you find it attached to the rest of the world." Such is the case with business, which is an intricate and interconnected web of relationships.

Unlike some businesses that believe they only exist to maximize return on investment for their shareholders, conscious businesses focus on their whole business ecosystem, creating and optimizing value for all of their stakeholders, understanding that strong and engaged stakeholders lead to a healthy, sustainable, resilient business.

They recognize that without employees, customers, suppliers, funders, supportive communities, and a life-sustaining ecosystem, there is no business. Conscious business is a win-win-win proposition, which includes a healthy return to shareholders.

3. Conscious Leadership

Robert Greenleaf, author of *Servant Leadership*, observed that "Good leaders must first become good servants." Conscious leaders focus on "we" rather than "me." They inspire, foster transformation, and bring out the best in those around them. They understand that their role is to serve the purpose of the organization, to support the people within the organization, and to create value for all of the organization's stakeholders. They recognize the integral role of culture and purposefully cultivate a conscious culture of trust and care.

4. Conscious Culture

"Culture eats strategy for lunch." Famed management guru Peter Drucker didn't mince words, and he knew how to identify and articulate the keys to success in business.

Culture is the embodied values, principles, and practices

underlying the social fabric of a business, which permeates its actions and connects the stakeholders to each other and to the company's purpose, people, and processes.

A conscious culture fosters love, care, and inclusiveness. It builds trust among the company's team members and all its other stakeholders. Conscious culture is an energizing and unifying force that truly brings a conscious business to life.

CONSUMERS WANT CONSCIOUS CAPITALISM

Andrew Hewitt, speaking at a Conscious Capitalism event in 2015, quoted a study that found that only "20 percent of brands worldwide are seen to meaningfully and positively impact people's lives, yet 91 percent of global consumers would switch brands if a different brand of similar price and quality supported a good cause.

"With this huge gap between societal values and corporate values, it's no wonder that purpose-driven organizations are far outperforming the pack. Doing good has become good business, not only because of changing consumer values but also because good companies are attracting the top talent, particularly millennials who are estimated to make up 75 percent of the global workforce by 2025."[3]

3 CONE, "2013 Cone Communications/ Echo Global CSR Study." http://www.conecomm.com/research-blog/2013-cone-communications-echo-global-csr-study.

To put it another way, human beings deserve more than a soul-sucking experience when they head to work. People can no longer be expected to get up every day and simply exist to meet a budget number. They also expect to be treated fairly, even get inspired.

Importantly, purpose also serves as a guiding light during the inevitable storms that face every business. If you think about 2008 to 2010, when the economy took a giant dive, businesses that had a strong sense of purpose did much better. People stuck with them despite the downturn.

MAINTAINING PURPOSE IN A CRISIS

Barry-Wehmiller is a multibillion-dollar, multinational engineering company that was hit extremely hard during the 2008 recession. But when business dropped by 40 percent, CEO Bob Chapman remembered the company purpose: "we measure success by the way we touch the lives of people."

Instead of doing massive layoffs, Chapman asked himself, "What would a responsible family do in this crisis?" The answer? Shared sacrifice. As a direct result of consulting its corporate purpose, the company created a furlough program whereby every person in the organization took four weeks of unpaid time off. They also suspended 401(k) matching.

According to Chapman, "The reaction was extraordinary. Some team members offered to take double furloughs so others would not be affected...Many welcomed the time off, scheduling it so they could spend summer home with children or participate in special volunteer projects."

Barry-Wehmiller emerged from the recession ahead of many others, and when orders picked up, performance ramped quickly. "Why?" asks Chapman. "Because our actions during a time of great distress didn't damage the cultural fabric of the company—like layoffs so often do—but rather strengthened it."[4]

In an era of shifting dynamics and changing markets, an era of chaos, uncertainty, and ambiguity in just about everything humans try, you have to have clarity in why you exist. You have to have a stable beacon of light on which you can focus, no matter what the weather conditions.

BUT DON'T FORGET THE BOTTOM LINE

Of course, no matter how conscious your capitalism, you still have to turn a profit. You cannot just happily focus on higher purpose and values and not do the work. Leaders, like everyone in the company, have to perform.

---

4 Bob Chapman, "How A Family Shared A Burden." https://www.trulyhumanleadership.com/?p=645.

That takes blocking and tackling. It takes resiliency and perseverance.

Budgets matter. Data points matter. Quarterly goals matter. But it's not either/or. It's not purpose or profits, values or growth. You can have both sides of the coin and put the coin in your pocket, too.

When you hire leaders, you need to find people who can effectively balance purpose and execution. That means putting them through a covert discovery process to understand their own purpose and their own values. But it also means understanding how they will drive the business forward from a functional standpoint. In the chapters to come, we will help you learn how to find leaders who can strike the balance within the confines of your company DNA.

But until you know that DNA, you're driving blind.

COMPANY CULTURE: THE WAY PEOPLE BEHAVE

Company culture can be hard to pin down. Do people contradict the boss in meetings, or do they not? Do people get opinions from other stakeholders before they make a decision, or do they not? Do they feel free to wear sandals? Are they sneered at if they wear a tie?

Every company has a culture—and a set of rituals—all its

own. At Unilever, we saw that Paul Polman has a ritual of sitting in on job interviews in whatever office he's visiting.

Here at Y Scouts, we have one ritual in which, each morning at 8:45, we meet to talk about what we're up to and what we are up against in our current projects. If people are out of the office, they connect through video conferencing. We call it the Morning Swarm, and it takes just fifteen minutes. People talk about the most important thing that happened the day before, what their top priorities are for the day, and where they may need help.

We are so conscious of our values and our Y Scouts Method that even as leaders, we feel completely comfortable saying to a coworker, "I got off track on that issue, and I was knocking everyone else off track as a result. I thought I was helping move people along, and then I realized I was working outside the Y Scouts Method."

No kidding, we talk like that. After such an admission, we will consciously turn to the relentless learning associated with admitting a mistake. Why? *Because one of our key values is "relentless growth."*

A CLARIFYING MOMENT

Humans are pack animals. We find joy and meaning in group undertakings and group survival. People naturally want to feel part of a group. They want to contribute and be a valued member of their tribe, their clan, their team.

History has shown the best human behavior comes out during the most trying times of tragedy and war—events that bring us together with our clans. We judge ourselves and others on how we act in these moments of crisis, when safety comes from an affirmation of the group and purpose becomes clear. In the days following 9/11, for example, suicide and depression rates plummeted in New York City.

Every pack has its unique DNA. A good leader will understand that DNA and foster it, increasing everyone's job satisfaction.

A good leader will also go to great lengths to protect company DNA when it's threatened.

PROTECTING THE PACK

A CEO recently told us about a clarifying moment at her company. It's a fast-growing firm trying to be a disruptor in its industry. It has based its internal culture on a huge amount of honesty and open communication. But because of the speed with which it hires, it sometimes pulls in people who don't necessarily get its culture or abide by its values.

Her tale about protecting the culture of the pack is worth repeating.

This CEO once hired a serious industry hotshot into a key leadership position. He was immediately productive and garnered rapid trust and admiration from the team. Trouble was, he was taking all kinds of shortcuts on company policies to get his results and lying about it to upper management.

When our client figured out what was going on, she fired him on the spot. Her goal? *Protect the culture of the pack.*

Because of the suddenness of this hotshot's departure, the CEO felt she had to immediately bring together the team and make an announcement. But at the meeting, another employee, who had become extremely loyal to the hotshot, had an utter meltdown about the decision. This woman—let's call her Tiffany—publicly blasted leadership's decision-making process in a way that could be hurtful and damaging to everyone's morale.

She said things like "I know you don't want to hear this, but I'm fucking pissed."

At that moment, the true meaning of the company's "honest and open communication" values became clear to everyone. Honest, yes; hurtful, no. Tiffany did not understand this, but everyone else saw it clearly. Within a couple of hours, Tiffany was also gone, and *the DNA had been preserved.*

Necessary decisions? Absolutely. Good company culture is vital and must be preserved. You must understand your culture, you must hire for the culture, and sometimes you must fire for the culture. It's part of your responsibility as a leader.

FINDING YOUR DNA

Before we conduct an executive search, Y Scouts must deeply understand a company's values, purpose, and culture. Otherwise, we can never achieve radical alignment and that best possible outcome.

Some companies have well-established values, along with mission statements that actually prove useful in understanding their purpose. In other words, their mission and values statements don't include crap like "At Acme Corp, our mission is to transform with insight, lead with innovation, and maximize potential value for our customers and stockholders."

Sometimes, when hiring for a key position, company leadership will find itself forced to go through some healthy soul-searching. Especially when it needs to find a leader who will *change* the company's corporate culture.

In any case, at Y Scouts, we refuse to drive blind. We insist on fanatical preparation. So we start with our DNA survey. You can, too.

THE SURVEY

Our organizational DNA survey seeks to understand the values of a company *that actually exist,* along with the behaviors that support those values within the corporate culture.

Even if a company has a written set of values that is actually distributed and actually used, context matters.

A company may say it requires "integrity."

Now, if you take four people and ask them to define "integrity," they might all come up with similar definitions. But dig deeper, and they may have completely different *behavioral standpoints* about how integrity should be manifested or actually is manifested in their company. If all four are working on the same team, you have a problem.

Put more simply, you can't simply ask, "Do you believe in

integrity?" You have to ask, "What does integrity in action mean right here and right now in your department?"

We run the DNA survey anonymously with ten or so carefully chosen people as a set of rather open-ended questions. The results often prove eye-opening for our clients, because the survey clarifies *what behaviors are actually occurring* on the ground in real time.

You must get real-time data, because values and culture evolve, often quickly. You can see an example of one of our surveys in the sidebar. Notice that the questions are designed so employees can't just spit back junk from the company handbook.

No matter how clearly defined the corporate culture, a DNA survey can be a valuable snapshot for a recruiting team before it sets out on the next step in the road to fanatical preparation: role definition.

Even better, the DNA survey may show that you have a hell of a lot of work to do to get your company on track, values-wise. If so, buy Ann Rhoades's book, *Built on Values,* and get cracking.

Y SCOUTS COMPANY DNA QUESTIONS

If your company disappeared, what would the world miss?

What three words best describe your company's culture?

What's the one thing you never want to see change in the culture of your company?

Please provide one or two examples of your company's core values in action.

What behaviors are most often recognized and rewarded? And how are those behaviors rewarded?

How, and how often, do you receive feedback regarding your performance?

If you could change only one thing about the culture your company, what would it be?

Thinking about the leaders in the company, how would you describe the organization's leadership style?

Is risk-taking encouraged at your company, and what happens when people fail?

CHAPTER 4

...Then Define the Role

If you have done the work of understanding your company's DNA, you're getting closer to knowing what kind of leader you need to hire. But you're not there yet. In fact, you need to clock plenty more time in the Department of Fanatical Preparation.

Like we said, hiring good leaders ain't easy. In this chapter, we will walk you through the rest of your fanatical prep, and then in chapter 5, you'll actually start talking to candidates.

DON'T CUT AND PASTE A JOB DESCRIPTION

After you understand your values and purpose, the next

step in the Y Scouts Method is to develop a holistic vision for the role. Notice that we did not say "job description." Why? Because JDs have become so riddled with clichés, redundancy, and bloated confusion that a new term is needed.

Just as importantly, a JD assumes that a job will not change. All jobs change, more quickly than ever these days. Roles evolve; JDs don't.

Traditionally, both company leaders and hiring managers do their best to task HR with filling positions; traditionally, the handoff is lame. So what happens? An HR person who isn't very familiar with the actual role ends up writing or rewriting a traditional JD. If no JD exists, they Google similar positions and then copy and paste together something long and usually irrelevant to the actual outcomes the role needs to deliver.

Warning: HR diligently practices "defensive job description." By including absolutely everything, they feel they are covering their asses. No one can say they didn't ask the sales VP for experience in configuring salesforce.com backend workflows, dammit! Never mind that a good VP would probably delegate that task.

As a result, the traditional JD grows into a laundry list of competencies and experience both absurdly lengthy and rarely accurate to the actual goals of the position. It's impossible to interview someone about twenty different qualifications, but lists of thirty-plus are not uncommon. Usually, both candidates and interviewers have to focus on the three to five issues that really matter; the rest are barely "checked off."

Many times, candidates have to figure out which of the qualifications are just cover-your-ass filler.

DEFINING SUCCESS

The first step to correctly defining a leadership role is to define success. But no one single person, including you, knows what success looks like for a given role. Seriously. Even if you own the whole business, you do not have enough perspective to define a role's success. Multiple stakeholders *always* exist for every role, and neither you nor the hiring manager—and especially not HR—should go at it alone.

Ideally, some folks from outside the organization who consistently interact with this role will also be consulted. Want to know the *true* success criteria for that new sales VP? Ask your sales team and your best customers. Be thoughtful, but cast the net as widely as reasonable.

A TYPICAL AND AWFUL LAUNDRY LIST JOB DESCRIPTION

Here's a typical, real, and ugly job description. As with most traditional JDs, it's way too long. No one could possibly have all these skills in exactly this manner, and no interviewer could possibly evaluate all these issues. Does this look familiar?

VP Sales Operations and Sales Support

This position is responsible for providing thought leadership and analytical guidance toward the achievement of determined sales and operational objectives. This position will provide input to and develop strategies in conjunction with Sales Managers and appropriate business development teams to determine how to best meet these objectives. This position is key in architecting action steps, analytics, and insights for internal and external customers. This position will lead a team of sales support personnel tasked with providing support to internal and external customers with regard to legal, compliance, regulatory issues, and requests for information/proposal. In addition, this role will monitor forecasts vs. budget, coordinate materials to support a sales and marketing function, and develop and execute sales training. This includes but is not limited to sales, planning, reporting, quota setting and management, process optimization, training and development, program development and implementation, compensation design and maintenance, contract management, and ownership of all CRM systems.

Essential Functions

- Collaborate with Sales and other business leaders to identify sales support opportunities and needs and develop strategies to support client retention, revenue, and strategic objectives.

- Develop and optimize operations strategies including inbound customer contacts, triage capabilities, and efficient issue resolution.

- Lead efforts in coordinating consistent Responses for RFI/RFPs.
- Lead a sales support organization that optimizes the process for internal risk approvals, contract management, key account reporting, and business review reporting.
- Evolve and manage an effective Salesforce.com strategy for the sales team.
- Develop comprehensive reporting tools relative to forecasting and actual results of the pipeline, lead generation, revenue, account development, and client growth/retention.
- Collaborate with Finance to perform monthly billing audit and commission calculations.
- Build, retain, and motivate highly engaged, high-performance teams through a demonstrated commitment to talent management and training.
- Engage and educate customers on service delivery through tools, analytics, and other means.
- Manage the CRM tool and provide reporting and analytics to sales teams and management.
- Analyze sales data; identify opportunities, concerns, and trends and recommend and support the implementation of actions to increase success.
- Work with Product teams to ensure training of the Sales team on the competitive landscape and industry trends.
- Maintain strong internal relationships and collaborate cross-functionally to ensure alignment of all internal partners.
- Comply with all security policies and procedures to ensure that the highest level of system and data confidentiality, integrity, and availability is maintained.

REQUIRED EXPERIENCE

Minimum Qualifications

- Education or experience equivalent to a Bachelor's degree in business, finance, or another related field
- Seven years business-to-business sales and/or sales operations experience in financial services or risk management
- In-depth knowledge of the financial services industry and risk management arena, and understanding of the competitive landscape of processors, credit bureaus, payment systems, fraud, risk, and compliance providers
- Strong understanding of the sales process, pipeline management, and forecasting sales performance
- Effective leadership skills and passion for building highly engaged, high-performance teams
- Ability to develop sales support strategies and business plans that drive revenue and produce measurable results
- Effective written, verbal, and public speaking skills
- Strong analytical and process skills
- Ability to create and deliver compelling and persuasive arguments with an executive level audience; comfort establishing new relationships with and influencing customers from the analyst up to the C Suite both internally and externally
- Ability to collaborate across the company to enhance operations and results—strong influencing skills
- Demonstrated success in growing revenue and market share in a competitive market
- Ability to travel to customer locations and industry events—

estimated travel 20–30 percent

- Approved background and drug screen are required.

Preferred Qualifications

- Experience in advanced analytics
- Experience leading sales teams
- Additional related education and/or experience preferred

Maybe you'll discover, for example, that your new sales VP will have to overcome an "unfriendliness" reputation your company has developed over the years. That might significantly change your hiring criteria.

Maybe your customer's input will help you recognize a specific competency or skillset that will help your company ignite new opportunities. Or even better, maybe the fact that you even asked for their opinion will open the door to a new relationship or revenue stream.

THE MULTI-STAKEHOLDER APPROACH

We once recruited a CFO for a midsized company. To adequately define success, we went and talked to the company's key banking contact.

That banker works with a host of CFOs and could answer

key questions like "What knowledge or attitudes constitute best-in-class for a CFO today?" Did the company's president or CEO know the full answer to that question? HR? No, of course not. Our conversation with the company's banker really clarified the issues for everyone.

Crucially, this key banker also felt happy and included in the process. In fact, by talking to the banker, the CEO learned that his company had been at risk of losing its line of credit because the last CFO hadn't been in compliance with sending the proper financials.

The moral of the story? Talk to stakeholders, wherever you find them.

This moral does not just apply to highly senior positions like CFO. Other positions may interact with important suppliers, customers, and vendors. Why not ask their opinions? Worst case, their opinions will be useless. But in every case, they will be happy you asked, and once again, you may solidify or expand some key relationships.

We guarantee that your stakeholders will feel much better about your eventual hire and more fully invested in that role's success, because you gathered their input. Stakeholders can and should also be included in the actual interview process, whether from a competency or a values alignment perspective. Not only will you get new insights, but you will also get buy-in from the exact people who must help the new person succeed.

Running a nonprofit? Absolutely involve your board members in key hires. It will keep you in touch with their success criteria and draw them closer to your organization.

CONSENSUS MATTERS

When you reach consensus among your stakeholders on an image of success, not only will you hire the right person to fulfill that image, but when the goals are achieved, stakeholders will view that achievement in the same way. When stakeholders have different views of success—especially when their views remain a mystery—the disparities can literally destroy the contributions made by a new hire.

You will also have a way to evaluate your new hire's efforts. Clearly outline success, and you can later ask, "What did we ask this person to achieve? Did this person achieve it?"

NO JOB IS AN ISLAND

Every role in your company depends on other roles for its success. Often, these other roles will have perspectives on defining success that the hiring manager could not possibly offer. A good role definition will take into account *all* these points of view. The Role Visioning Survey discussed in this chapter helps gather those points of view.

KEEPING IT SHORT AND SIMPLE

It may seem counterintuitive, but multi-stakeholder approaches actually lead to simpler role definitions and more enticing Opportunity Profiles given to candidates; we'll explain the structure of this new kind of document in a moment. That's because such approaches better avoid those generic, copy-paste laundry lists created by HR and focus on clear, understandable, and inspiring goals.

Your definitions of success should boil down to only three to five clear outcomes. No matter how complex the role—including president or CEO—we never use more than five total success outcomes in our scouting and hiring processes. All key responsibilities can fall under these outcomes, and success should be tied to specific time frames: a year, six months, even ninety days. You can see a sample set of success outcomes here, as an excerpt of a full Opportunity Profile, which can be found in appendix A.

A short, simple set of success criteria will *always* attract better candidates, because exceptional leaders see an opportunity to exercise leadership in creative ways. Success criteria also lead to a far more palatable interview process, which can now focus on both performance and values.

SAMPLE SUCCESS OUTCOMES AND KEY RESPONSIBILITIES: HEAD OF PRODUCT

Role Summary:

The Head of Product will be a collaborative and results-oriented Product Management leader with proven experience prioritizing and executing product innovations that provide incredible value to the end user. As the Head of Product, this person will use the best available data and market conditions to guide [Company] on its mission to deliver world-class products that empower users and their teams to [purpose of the company].

Success Outcome #1:

Discover and create efficiencies that enable consistent, high-quality delivery of consulting services leveraging a formalized, scalable "Consulting Framework" to drive a 90+ percent retention rate and at a 30:1 client to Customer Success Consultant ratio capability.

Key Responsibilities:

- Drive consultant enablement products that achieve a 90+ percent retention rate and a 30:1 client to consultant ratio capability.
- Capture and write user stories and requirements accurately, clearly, and efficiently.
- Collaborate with VP of Customer Success to craft and communicate a compelling product vision that energizes and inspires the organization.
- Create a well-defined roadmap and execution plan for operationalizing and integrating the Consulting Framework into the customer experience.
- Collaborate with various departments and stakeholders to co-create a content roadmap associated with delivering the framework.

Success Outcome #2:

Iterate and evolve existing components of our new Analytics Platform: collaborate with VP Product Technology, VP Customer Success, third-party vendors, and SMEs to execute design cleanup and simplification of the platform.

Key Responsibilities:

- Improve analytics dashboards including metrics viewed by the user, including but not limited to A/R, Scheduling, Treatment Planning, and Production in alignment with the SPS Enhancements Theme.

- Establish a transparent roadmap and consistent release cycle through working with VP Customer Success, VP Product Technology, and VP of Growth.

- Create and integrate key performance indicators (KPIs) including Customer Health Score and Client ROI.

- Tackle big problems and deliver significant customer benefit by planning to release solution components on a regular basis.

- Work with VP Customer Success to define upcoming renewal strategy aligned with a long-term pricing approach.

Success Outcome #3:

Actively contribute to a high-performance culture of innovation and collaboration. As [Company] evolves into a product-and-technology-centric company, this teammate will participate in and contribute to the development of a world-class culture of innovation.

Key Responsibilities:

- Actively participate in the sharing of ideas, research, and best practices across various disciplines.

- Maintain an "always be recruiting" mindset, identifying "A-Players" and introducing them to the team.
- Facilitate and strengthen cross-departmental collaboration and internal communications.

When the interviews roll around, you can ideally spread out success outcomes and associated responsibilities among different interviewers so everyone's not repeating themselves—another common problem. Focus a single interviewer on one or two of your success outcomes, and they can really dig in. They can also compare candidates without juggling dozens of variables. It's humanly impossible to keep fifteen to twenty criteria front and center while conducting an interview or making a decision. The human mind simply does not work that way.

Okay, now how do you actually come up with those three to five key success criteria? At Y Scouts, we do another survey.

ENVISIONING OR RE-ENVISIONING ROLES

The biggest danger when defining success outcomes is everyone's tendency to look backward. Most people ask, "What would a good VP of sales have done over the last two years to have made those last two years better?" Unfortunately, those qualities and initiatives might not at all apply to the next two years—another big reason to throw out old JDs.

As companies grow, most hit a leadership wall. Having a process to define what success looks like six to twenty-four months out can surmount that wall.

Just remember that at the pace that the world is changing today, it's a fool's errand to predict what a role will need to deliver beyond two years. The good news? If you find quality people who share your values and are authentically aligned with your purpose, you can make future changes to what they need to deliver.

As long as you have alignment with a new leader, you will find a willingness on their part to lean in and learn.

If people come in with a fixed mindset or aren't aligned with a mission, as soon as the job becomes something they didn't sign up for, problems emerge.

As Steve Jobs famously said, "We hire really smart people and then get out of their way."[5] Getting out of their way includes not blocking the road with a stale JD.

---

5 Marcel Schwantes, "Steve Jobs Once Gave Some Brilliant Management Advice on Hiring Top People. Here It Is in 2 Sentences." https://www.inc.com/marcel-schwantes/this-classic-quote-from-steve-jobs-about-hiring-employees-describes-what-great-leadership-looks-like.html.

GETTING THE COMPLETE FORWARD VIEW

In order to define success for a specific role, Y Scouts performs an exercise called "role visioning." It's an effort to look forward instead of backward. We send our Role Visioning Survey to three to six important stakeholders, and from there we get to our focused success outcome profile for the role.

Specific "responsibilities" are avoided. Why? It's silly to assume that the specific block-and-tackle responsibilities of a role aren't going to change, given the rate at which all business changes. Role visioning allows us to get out of the minutiae and focus on big issues. We also tend to get some useful honesty.

Here's an example of a typical Role Visioning Survey:

1. What is your working relationship with this role?
2. Hiring the right person for this role will lead to what/where?
3. What are the three most important initiatives/projects/objectives this role is expected to ignite or complete? Please describe each in detail.
4. Looking at the three initiatives/projects/objectives you identified, what metrics or key performance indicators should we use to measure/track the success of each?
5. How long should each of the three initiatives/projects/

objectives take to fully achieve, and what factors may influence this timeline?

6. What proof points should the ideal candidate have in their prior experience that would give us confidence in their ability to successfully achieve these three initiatives/projects/objectives?
7. If you decided to hire someone from outside of your industry, which industry or industries offer the highest probability of skills-based or experiential transferability?
8. Please share alternative job titles and/or specific companies you would target for this search.
9. Who are you REALLY looking for in this role?
10. What will you admire most about the right person for this role?
11. How will your role and performance be impacted when the right person is successful in this position?

These surveys are given out individually—never in group sessions. You must avoid groupthink at all costs. If you bring all the stakeholders into one room and start asking these questions, the same person who always comes up with the ideas, or has the highest rank, will end up defining the role. Important new ideas might even be laughed at.

Why not just pass around a draft JD for everyone to mark up and add their opinions? Because starting with a JD automatically prejudices the process, snuffing out new ideas and perspectives. Instead of creating the freedom to envision what could be, you get a look backward. You also get laziness—people just won't do the serious thinking you need them to do.

Our surveys take only twenty to thirty minutes to answer and always prove incredibly valuable.

COLLECTING RESPONSES

When you get back your responses, take some serious time to look for common themes and areas of disagreement. Also look for opportunities.

In Max's brother's company, when it set out to hire a new head of marketing, the Role Visioning Survey surfaced a lot of disagreements about what this person should be spending time on. Should this role be about rainmaking or leading the rainmakers?

The company saw how it absolutely had to understand its success criteria before going out to hire for the role.

CONTEXT MATTERS

When you create a role using a role visioning process, you are hiring not for a title but for a *context*. And context matters. A recent article in the *Harvard Business Review* assembled lots of data on hiring techniques and concluded that hires made within the context of success outcomes had the most chance of, well, succeeding.[6]

Some examples of contextual challenges identified by HBR included the following:

- Is the company newly leading in a global or cross-cultural set of a team environment?
- Is the company transforming a very high-conflict culture?
- Is the company being led through a merger or acquisition process?
- Is the company, due to unforeseen circumstances, now being operated with a high set of resource restraints?
- Is it about growing the business through innovation?
- Is it about growing the business through market share?
- Is it about growing the business through cost competitiveness?

Different leaders will approach each of these challenges very differently. It's not about titles; it's about whether your company can align with someone on those

6 Harvard Business Review, "When Hiring Execs, Context Matters Most." https://hbr.org/2017/09/when-hiring-execs-context-matters-most.

approaches. In that sense, it's a lot more about the experience than skills. You don't want to bring in someone whose resume looks amazing but who has never dealt with the level of challenges or number of variables your company faces.

Skills and experience are very different things. Finding an executive who has successfully dealt with similar contexts in the past may well outweigh a specific skillset.

Imagine for a moment that you are a manufacturing company and you cannot grow without some major cost-reduction initiatives. Don't become focused on finding a manufacturing industry exec with impeccable credentials "who has grown a company." That's simply not enough context. Did the exec grow a previous company through mergers and acquisitions but was never forced to stay competitive through cost reduction? Their experience might be meaningless for your context.

IDENTIFYING THE PACE OF A JOB

Understanding what we call the *pace* of a job may be a huge factor in contextualizing a challenge, finding the right person, and having that person understand what they're heading into.

Suppose you are a construction company looking for

someone who has experience working up estimates on building large commercial structures.

To perform that job, candidates have to learn how to interact with architects, finance departments, and the like. In such a situation, everyone can easily misunderstand *pace.* That previous COO of a construction company you are thinking of hiring may have worked on huge structures. She may have interacted with all these kinds of departments and suppliers. But how many projects did she handle at once?

A candidate who is used to handling five projects at a time will have a very different experience than one who handled fifteen projects at a time. That difference is *pace.* With more customers come more stakeholders, and that makes time frames more and more critical. But plenty more factors create *pace.* In some companies, the COO may meet with the CEO only quarterly. In another company, they may meet every day.

The example of the overly corporate fellow named Jackson we detailed in the introduction could be considered a mismatch of pace. Brian was growing his startup, Jobing.com, at a furious pace. He thought he needed an executive with B-school chops who knew about scale. But he hired a B-school guy from the pharmaceutical industry who was used to working at a completely different pace.

It takes years to get a drug through the FDA and out to market. It takes minutes to update a SaaS site. Jackson had the executive-level gravitas, but he could not adapt to the pace.

The key factor of pace should have been discovered *up front,* through developing clear success criteria and a truly useful Ideal Candidate Profile, which we will discuss shortly.

OKAY, BUT WHAT ABOUT THOSE SKILLS?

So far, we haven't talked much in this chapter about "skillsets." And certainly, it's true that traditional JDs are littered with highly specific, often required experiences and skills.

But here's the honest truth: *someone with a totally different set of skills and experience than the last person who held the position, or someone with a different set of skills than you at first imagine, may be able to achieve your success outcomes better. Much better.*

Why does that happen so often? Because the overall problem of *incremental improvement*, which we have come to understand historically in relation to companies, applies to people as well. You will find great *workers* who advance incrementally in their skills throughout their lives. But great *leaders* rarely rise through incremental advancement.

The problem of promoting the most-decorated sailor to the position of captain applies when you recruit from the outside as well. When you focus your search on skills, you often eliminate leaders with fabulous talents, passions, and values. That means you can end up with some awfully skillful person who totally fails to lead.

DON'T GIVE THE ANSWERS IN ADVANCE

All that said, we know that the leadership role you are looking to fill will require some clear "table stakes." You will need to work those into a different document, your Ideal Candidate Profile. The profile will serve as an *internal-only* guide for your hiring team.

Do not publish the "required skillsets" in a JD. By making and publishing lists of highly specific experiences and skills in a JD, you are not only boxing yourself into a specific type of background, but you are also practically begging candidates to adapt their resumes—and interview responses—to fit the model you have provided.

Do traditional JDs actually lead candidates to lie? Well, let's just say that skills that didn't exist before often magically appear on resumes, just when needed. Statistics show that about 85 percent of people lie on their resumes—a fact we'll discuss in more detail later.

For now, think about it this way: by publishing lists of required skills, you are giving the candidate the answers to the test in advance. Candidates are smart. They can think of ways to demonstrate those skills, even if they don't exist. When you've divulged the exam answers, it's virtually impossible to untangle fact from fiction during interviews.

Suppose you're really hoping your new VP of sales has significant Salesforce.com skills. If you put "Extensive Salesforce.com experience required" on your job description, we can pretty much guarantee that every resume you receive will mention Salesforce experience. It's likely that half of those resumes never mentioned Salesforce before.

"Gee," thinks the candidate, "I used Salesforce a few times. And anyway, I can watch a couple of YouTube demos for the gist. That way, I can at least get through the first interview cut."

Indeed, your tedious list of twenty-plus skills has made bogus strategies like this pretty much a requirement for all your candidates.

WRITING THE OPPORTUNITY PROFILE

As we said, we don't like the term "job description." The term "Opportunity Profile" helps everyone understand that a leadership role represents an opportunity for a company to move forward, too.

Every role is just as much an opportunity for a company as it is for a candidate.

When a candidate sees your short, success-oriented Opportunity Profile, they may be surprised to find it doesn't talk about skills at all. But fear not: people can self-select on the basis of the success outcomes listed in the Opportunity Profile, just fine.

In our Opportunity Profiles, we try not to focus on job titles, as they can be misleading and can quickly turn away otherwise qualified candidates. Why? Because many candidates don't at first see their experience aligning with a specific title.

By focusing on success outcomes, both you and your potential candidates can see well beyond a job title. In fact, sometimes the outcome-based view allows you to identify a more appropriate title for the role.

SURPRISING ALIGNMENTS DISCOVERED

We once worked with a behavioral health company that ran a chain of high-end drug treatment centers. They were looking for a general manager-type role, but in their industry, that's called a clinical manager. When they posted for clinical manager, they received few responses. After we took them through our Y Scouts process, we realized they were seeking what's usually called a chief operating officer (COO) or operations leader. Clinical managers are licensed, but in this case, no license was required.

In the end, we found a candidate who had awesome experience running large, franchised restaurant chains—highly relevant experience, when you think about it. Coincidentally, when we took this candidate through our process, we discovered that running drug treatment centers was a kind of dream job for him. Why? He had lost his brother to a serious drug problem, and he really wanted to make a difference for others.

Such a radical alignment, based on a candidate's personal passion, could never have been discovered with a traditional JD posting/resume evaluation process.

Essentially, we put the success outcomes before the title.

This company needed someone to run geographically

dispersed, locally managed operations flawlessly. They didn't need someone who knew all about drug treatment techniques.

BEING HONEST

When companies lie about themselves, candidates lie about themselves. Result: unhappiness.

Companies will always try to paint their company DNA in the best light when they write a public document like an Opportunity Profile. But you will find it far more beneficial to be transparent about the challenges you face, even in your company culture, because you will find people who want to be part of solving those challenges. Lay your cards on the table so everyone acts from a place of authenticity.

Looking for a marketing director? Why not say, "We're behind the curve in social media, and we need someone to get us *ahead* of the curve." Looking for an operations director? How about "We've been growing so fast we've started losing control of our workflows. We need someone to define and enforce processes."

If a company position advertises itself as nothing but sunshine and rainbows, candidates will be annoyed and shocked when they find out otherwise. Be honest so you and your new hire can become a team, tackling the issues from day one.

EFFECTIVE ONBOARDING

Good onboarding may be the most disastrously neglected piece of the recruiting puzzle. Every day of the first week should be planned out. And every minute of the first day. If you don't already have an onboarding process defined for a leadership position when you make the call to offer the job, it's too late. You're toast.

Onboarding actually begins way back during the first interaction between the candidate and the employer. That very first email or call you make to start the conversation, well before any interviews occur. Every interaction from that moment on defines expectations, values, purpose, and culture, right from the first "hello."

If the candidate has a shitty hiring experience, they will expect shittiness when they get in the door. Because culture is largely about people imitating one another, shittiness might define their entire tenure on the job.

You cannot treat people one way during recruiting and then shift to another way when they are hired. As a leader yourself, you are defining how feedback is given, how input is received, how roles impact different stakeholders. Your new hire must understand all this and understand it within the success outcomes they will take on.

That first day must be planned with intentional precision, because it will be remembered forever and set the tone for everything to come. Who will the candidate meet? What will be said to whom?

How will you make sure the experience is smooth as silk so that on their way home, your new hire actually celebrates? When their significant other asks, "How was your first day?" how will they respond? Make sure their answer is a hearty, "It was amazing. I actually can't wait to go back in tomorrow." Not, "Kind of confusing, but I guess I'll figure it out."

Later, if you misrepresent the job or the company during the interview process, the truth will also come out quickly. This happens so often that people practically expect to be misled and may be pleasantly surprised to find you were being honest. At Y Scouts, we've had the joy of hearing people say, "You guys made your culture sound so great that I was expecting a bomb to drop on the first day. But you guys really do care about each other, just like you said."

INTERNAL-ONLY IDEAL CANDIDATE PROFILE

Every Y Scouts Opportunity Profile includes a paired, internal-only document. We call it the Ideal Candidate Profile. The Ideal Candidate Profile *does* list the skills everyone believes a role requires, and that doc will be used by everyone in the process *except the candidate.*

Do all these steps and documents demand way more work than cutting and pasting together a JD? Yes. The Y Scouts process takes longer than the traditional process, and it can seem frustrating to feel that you are "starting over" with each key hire. But that's a good thing. Role definitions must constantly evolve, just as business strategies must be revisited. So must your picture of your ideal candidate, as we can see in the sample here, shown fully in appendix B.

SAMPLE SKILLS REQUIRED TO SUCCEED: CHIEF INFORMATION OFFICER

Role Summary:

The Chief Information Officer (CIO) will assess, integrate, develop, deliver, and document systems software applications, architectural design, roadmap, and strategy. The CIO ultimately will be a champion of people and processes, creating clarity and consistency across the board while reducing friction and delivering a truly high-quality and delightful experience for both employees and customers. This role serves as a member of the leadership team, reports directly to the President, and must exemplify [Company]'s Core Values while working collaboratively across multiple functions, including IT, Operations, and Finance leadership.

Success Outcome #1

Strategic Leadership: Through a partnership with the President and organizational leadership, translate a strategic vision into tangible priorities, goals, and timelines to drive predictability in day-to-day operations and excellence in execution.

As evidenced by:

- At least fifteen years of professional success in roles of increasing responsibility, at least ten years of which will include leadership of high-performance teams.
- Proven track record of leading process integration, implementation, and change management.
- Specific examples of driving winning solutions with a positive outlook; takes responsibility, learns from failure, and embraces uncertainty.
- Sense of urgency; makes it happen and does the right thing; must be a team player who owns issues and acts and strives to be the best.

- Evidence of a strong working knowledge of data analysis and performance/operation metrics; will be practiced in data-focused decision-making and problem-solving.

Success Outcome #2

Execution: Deliver immediate value to our team by assessing, owning, and driving existing business/tech initiatives to success.

As evidenced by:

- Proven examples of selecting and implementing new ERP and/or Operating systems.
- Technically proficient in Microsoft Azure, SQL, Sharepoint, Great Plains (GP), Dynamics 365, ERP, CRM, and Salesforce.
- Deep understanding of project management methodologies and best practices. PMP and/or Six Sigma certification preferred.
- Experience working with IT teams to develop a continuous improvement program for all IT hardware, software, and operating systems to maximize efficiency and cost savings.

Success Outcome #3

Culture: Successful Integration with [Company], including the executive team, employees, and customers. Exemplify core values, champion our culture, and lead by example.

As evidenced by:

- Family-centered; must demonstrate family values and understand the need for balance.
- Reputation- and relationship-centered; a focus on doing the right thing with integrity, trustworthiness, and honesty; does what s/he says and goes the extra mile; demonstrates a willingness to help.

- Customer service mentality; innately demonstrates that customers are at the center of all we do; sense of urgency; follow-up; professional and respectful; adds value; consistently meets or exceeds expectations.
- Strong managerial credentials; will bring outstanding organizational and leadership abilities; proven examples of building and developing high-performing teams.
- Outstanding professional references from leaders, colleagues, and direct reports.

Drives Results: The US market has seen stagnant growth in recent years and needs a leader to reignite this growth with a relentless focus on product innovation and sales success. Coming into the company, they will quickly set priorities and ensure everyone from senior leadership to the front line understands the priorities and focuses on meeting their goals. They are driven by goals and achievement but able to do it in a way that helps people feel successful, empowered, and proud to be part of a high-performing organization.

Develops People: Although many leaders can achieve revenue and profit growth in the short term, exceptional leaders realize that accomplishments are only achieved through empowered and aligned team members. They spend significant time on team development and coaching, delegating the details of the work to their senior leaders to focus on helping the company maximize its impact. This leader values culture first and understands that when everyone is rowing in the same direction, anything is possible.

Learns Relentlessly: In the twenty-first century, learning crushes knowing as the world changes at a progressively faster pace. This individual has proof points in their life and their career that demonstrate curiosity and efforts to expand their knowledge base as often as possible. In addition, they are able to synthesize the information into their understanding of the world and its systems—they are open to changing their opinions and perspectives based on what they are learning.

Your current process probably focuses mostly on titles, just as your org chart probably focuses mostly on boxes. But titles tell only a small part of the story about the success outcomes and personality profiles needed in a role. As in the case of the treatment center chain, titles can be downright misleading and prevent you from finding the great leader you need.

Opportunity Profiles and Ideal Candidate Profiles each arise out of the fanatical preparation that has been done on values and role visioning. In the appendices, we offer examples of these documents, created by Y Scouts on behalf of our clients. All are focused on success outcomes, and all have led to some great hires.

In the next chapter, we'll dig into the formal Interview Guides.

DON'T LET CANDIDATES DEFINE OUTCOMES

We need to step back here to mention another sand trap in the recruiting process.

Often, hiring managers do not understand job descriptions as well as the candidates themselves do. That puts the hiring manager at a serious disadvantage. They often get bowled over in interviews because they don't have the right questions or find themselves unclear on success outcomes for a given position.

The higher the position, the more critical this danger becomes. When you hire at the C-level, you may think, "Hey, the person who is going to be running a company at that level should be able to diagnose my situation and decide whether they are the right person to fix it!"

In other words, you are leaving the setting of success outcomes and role visioning to the candidate. Indeed, the traditional way of hiring leads directly to this problem, especially when hiring is delegated too far down the chain. Why? Because a charismatic individual can blow plenty of smoke into the eyes of an unprepared hiring manager.

You must be intentional about clarifying a role before you begin recruiting. You and your stakeholders need to define success and look for alignment. This is your job even if you feel your company has become rudderless. Even if you are seeking a CEO to define a new path. Even if you do not trust your own knowledge.

Remember that you have a network of stakeholders to help determine whether candidates can meet the current and future needs of your company as well as align with your values. Don't let the candidate decide for you.

RIGHT AND WRONG RESUME SCANNING

We'll talk more about the problem with resumes later on, but you have already learned that resumes are not the be-all and end-all of alignment. You have also learned that skillsets should not define leadership positions. That means the computer technology now used to scan resumes for alignment will often suck.

We're not saying to avoid scanning entirely. In fact, if you just manually look at resumes for black-and-white keyword matches, you might as well use a computer program to make the first cut. Just remember that your computer will never recognize many of the potential alignments or commonalities that might very well end up making your business thrive.

Scan or no scan, use the resume only as a very brief snapshot of what somebody has accomplished. Always remember that a resume does not tell you who a candidate really is, where their values lie, and where they want to go.

In fact, at the time of this writing, when we are seeing low unemployment and high competition for leaders, we are finding that many of the best purpose-driven leaders haven't written out a resume in years. These days, if people have fully articulated resumes, it means they are "looking for work," and that's not necessarily important.

The majority of leaders we reach out to just want to provide a brief outline or profile, and often that's just fine.

A POSITIVE EXAMPLE OF SCANNING

Scanning can sometimes prove super helpful, but only if used properly.

A few years ago, a nonprofit was expanding its operation in the Phoenix area. Its mission was to help underserved populations graduate high school and go to college. Although the enterprise was organized and operated as a nonprofit, it was a firm believer that its best leaders would come from the for-profit world.

Nevertheless, when this organization asked Y Scouts to help them find a new executive director, it also knew that a traditional, profit-oriented executive wouldn't be quite enough. As a nonprofit, it had to make sure the values and purpose alignments were rock solid.

In this case, we did leverage technology to specifically scan resumes and profiles of for-profit leaders on social media and elsewhere. But we scanned for leaders who were also members of nonprofit boards focused on education and youth. That helped us find someone who's still in that role today.

GOING LOOKING

As you see, *we scan to search, not to sift.* And we search well beyond the net.

After decades in this business, we've come to the undeniable conclusion that waiting for people to apply to job ads is a very risky, if not hopeless, strategy. Instead, we use the power of technology to go out and identify the leadership profiles we believe contain the right mix of experiences and skills, and then we engage those leaders in a way that recognizes their gifts and talents. We don't wait for them to engage with us.

Yes, this is a lot more work. But that work will pay off. Somewhere along the line, the term "recruiting" eroded into a strangely passive verb—implying little more than shuffling through resumes. Real recruiting is about knowing whom you are looking for and owning up to the responsibility of proactively searching out and contacting those people.

The internet has made proactive searching far easier. You can quickly utilize social media platforms like LinkedIn, Facebook, Instagram, etc.—everyone today is findable, and the automated search tools are out there to help.

Recruiting means actively engaging people at conferences and other industry events and socializing at church, sports events, and peer groups. It means joining boards of organizations and participating in economic councils—getting out there and shaking hands.

If you are an executive at a growing company, you may already realize that you can never stop recruiting, wherever you are and whatever you are doing. But when you go out prepared with a good Ideal Candidate Profile, you know exactly what you're looking for. You're going to do your proactive work a whole lot better.

OUTPLAYING LADY LUCK

Before we move to a deeper discussion of leadership qualities and how to identify people who actually have those qualities, we'd like to invite you to reflect on the hiring choices you've made in the past.

Ask yourself, "How big a part did luck play in my previous searches? And how many times did that luck turn sour?"

How many times did you say, "How could we have known this person would be such a jerk?" Or "Somehow he got focused on all the wrong things, right from day one."

Now imagine you had involved multiple stakeholders to define success, re-envision the role, and create an Ideal Candidate Profile. Suppose you'd said, "Screw the job boards; let's actively recruit people for this role who not only have the skills and experience but also show an authentic alignment with our DNA."

Would Lady Luck still have come to sit in on the game? Sure. But think how your odds would have improved when it came time to lay down your hand.

PART II

Choosing Leaders

CHAPTER 5

Identifying the Right Leaders

You have armed yourself with a Values Blueprint, an Opportunity Profile, and an Ideal Candidate Profile. You feel fanatically prepared. But how will you actually identify great leaders when you see them? Or, because we're all about being specific, *how do you find leaders who will be great for your organization?*

You have already learned that the professional competencies required for a leadership position are nothing more than table stakes. So how do you move on to achieve radical alignment?

At Y Scouts, we go looking for people with the Ideal Candidate Profile, and then we focus right in on values, purpose, and culture. *Yup, right off the bat.* You should do the same—after all that work clarifying your company DNA, it's time to make it matter.

In the traditional hiring process, stuff like values, purpose, and culture comes as an afterthought. Truly just "nice to haves," barely mentioned after all the other boxes have been checked. Somewhere around the last three minutes of the third interview. But if you have been reading all our cautionary tales, starting with lovable Jay Cutler, you may now recognize that you actually have to *start* by understanding these qualities in your candidate.

At Y Scouts, after we've checked on the basics, we try to zoom right past the resume to the real person. Because that real person will need to display real leadership.

SEEKING ALIGNMENT UP FRONT

Most organizations have no qualifying process to determine whether their DNA aligns with a leader. None. Not at any point in the hiring cycle. As a result, candidates pretty much do their own discovery work. It's generally *up to the candidates* to figure out how people treat each other in your organization. What your people care about. Whether the culture will be "tolerable" for them.

Kind of nuts, when you think about it.

Of course, many candidates don't really try to answer these "soft" questions any more than the people doing the hiring do. Most candidates rush right into a job with a bare minimum of inquiry. "Is this company stable or growing? Is it the right title? Is it a step up?"

At some point, again near the *end* of a formal interview, they might tentatively ask you, "So, uh, what's the general atmosphere around here? Good team spirit? Competitive?" To which they usually get a meaningless reply.

Often, candidates don't even attempt to find out whether your company operates in a way that is consistent with the way they like to operate and with what matters most to them. They may even think it offensive to ask a question like "What sorts of behaviors are recognized and rewarded at this company?"

TAKING OFF THE MASKS

If you are going to find out the truth about a candidate, you have to go about your investigation intentionally and thoroughly.

At Y Scouts, we start with an informal conversation that does not reveal the title of the job or even the identity of the client. Admittedly, as a third party, we have a massive advantage in this quest. Because we do not post jobs but rather reach out to potential candidates we think might be worthwhile, we can approach them in a way that does not lead to BS.

When we don't reveal the client's identity or the specific job title, we eliminate the always-present temptation for a candidate to say what they think we want to hear. When people don't know the right answer or how to game a conversation, they often tell the truth. They cannot simply research our client and parrot back some analyst or redesign themselves on the spot.

Result: everyone speaks without masks.

THAT FIRST, INFORMAL CONVERSATION

After we've worked with our clients to create a detailed Opportunity Profile that includes company DNA and success outcomes, along with an Ideal Candidate Profile with proof points, we're ready to start a search.

Because we have a solid idea of what kind of leader we are looking for and where we might find them, why waste time posting a JD and getting a bunch of random replies with tailored resumes?

Instead, we make a target list and usually first reach out via email. In that email, we'll say something like, "We're representing a purpose-driven organization that is looking to add a leader to its team, and by the looks of your background, you appear to have many of the skills and experiences the role requires. But before we talk about the specific title and company, we'd like to invite you to spend some time with us, to give us the opportunity to get to know you the person, not you the resume."

If the candidate responds and we get to a first call, we start by explaining our approach. "As we look for great leaders for this client, we follow a fundamental philosophy in which we search not just for the right skills but also for serious alignment on values, purpose, and other important cultural aspects. We think the right alignment matters a lot.

"We know it sounds a bit unorthodox, but we actually *start* by talking with folks about their *own* purpose and values, along with their dreams and desires.

"In this first conversation, you will have to trust us that we wouldn't be reaching out if we didn't think we had a serious opportunity for you. But there's no point in getting into the size of the company, or the purpose of the company, or the exact title if it doesn't align with what matters most to you. So we'd like to simply talk about *you* and find out whether it would make sense for us to share more about the opportunity. Are you willing to spend thirty minutes with us to go through that discovery process?"

We find that the best people out there actually love these inquiries. No one has approached them this way in the past or ever even asked them about what matters most to them in a job. If they balk at talking about stuff like values and purpose, well, they're probably not a fit.

EXCEPTIONAL LEADERS GET IT

This approach was more challenging when we started in 2012. As we write today, exceptional leaders are in such short supply that they are not out there looking for work. They are looking for purpose. They are looking for meaning. And they're often thrilled that someone wants to talk about those subjects.

Job offers get thrown at exceptional people all the time: "Here's the company, the title, the dollars...Interested?" Such offers become just noise. But a discussion about values and purpose? Way cool.

We continually receive positive feedback on the way we engage with candidates on the front end. Some of the best and most frequent feedback from these leaders? The conversation "felt different," and that was one of the main reasons they responded. Our unusual conversation starter really moved the needle on their interest.

That's a huge advantage in an employment market currently yielding the lowest unemployment percentage in years, maybe even decades.

THE RIGHT QUESTIONS

In that first conversation, as in later interviews, our questions center not on previous responsibilities, years of employment, sales numbers, etc., but on concrete and specific examples of past *behavior.*

Unlike many interviewers, we only ask for *real* examples of struggles and leadership from their experience, not hypotheticals. Values questions never propose crap like, "What would you do if everyone hated someone you hired?" We're pretty sure that all "what if" questions are a waste of effort, because you are only learning whether the candidate can figure out what you want to hear.

We like to start with the question, "What do you care about most, both inside and outside of work?" Right off, the candidate knows they're heading into a very different kind of recruiting conversation. Often, it takes them a few seconds to get the hang of it and realize that we actually care about answers to questions like that. But then they warm up.

If the candidate comes back with an answer like, "Well, I mostly love to work," it's up to us to dig deeper. This person might find it a challenge to get through the rest of the interview, because they haven't thought through what really matters to them.

If the candidate replies, "My family matters most to me," as many do, we try to find out why. Seriously. We try to get them into details and see whether they've *thought through* the concept of family. If we have to prod them too much, maybe they haven't really defined their own values.

Often, we'll ask about upbringing—you can learn a great deal by the way a candidate discusses their upbringing and how it formed their character.

If a candidate keeps trying to maneuver the conversation back to their canned "skills speech," we know we might not be talking to someone who can handle the responsibility of being a leader and conversing on higher issues. We really need people who know how they derive the most meaning inside and outside of work.

WHY THIS WORKS

Most people like to talk about themselves and don't take too much prodding after they know it's okay. Tell them you are actually interested in their personal lives, and they'll sometimes go on for ten minutes about their origins and personal challenges. It can be very moving.

Here's our list of questions for that first conversation. The list is short and the questions open-ended so people have the space to talk and expand. We love that.

1. Tell me what you most care about both personally and professionally.
2. How did your upbringing shape you as a person and leader?
3. What do you enjoy doing in your life now that makes you the happiest?
4. What one or two values would you never compromise, and why?
5. Tell me about two of your most challenging life experiences. How have they shaped you as a person and leader?
6. What is it that you do naturally better than almost anyone else?
7. What's a major sacrifice you've made as a leader?

Genuine leaders—the kind of people you want in your organization—will have reflected on these issues in their lives. They will display the kind of self-awareness and thoughtfulness you need. They will not have focused only on skillsets and responsibilities, so they will actually be able to have this conversation with you, unprepared.

Later you can drill down into skillsets. Later you can talk responsibilities. But truly, when it comes to leadership, those are the cart that must follow the horse. Some other fruitful questions might be the following:

1. When do you feel most engaged and thriving in your work?
2. What are you not interested in doing?
3. If you could do anything and get paid what you're paid now, what would you do?

Remember how we told you we once recruited a guy who ran big restaurant chains to run a chain of drug treatment centers? We asked question 10 during our first informal conversation, in which we never mentioned the job we were hiring for. When he said, "If I could do anything I wanted and get paid for it, I'd work on running great drug treatment centers."

Damn! We got chills.

Ten questions are actually too many. If a first conversation goes well, you will only have to ask two or three open-ended questions, and the candidate will tell you everything that matters to them—their strengths, their weaknesses, what they like in an office, what they dislike in an office, their dream job, what they do in their free time. The works.

If they won't open up during a conversation like this, then

frankly, we're not interested. It likely means they're the type of person who does not believe an employer should understand them or care about their values and purpose. And by extension, they shouldn't care about a company's values and purpose either.

If the candidate immediately starts bitching and complaining openly about their current position, you should also consider that a red flag. A genuine leader will not do that. Watch out for these other areas of concern that signal a need to dive deep and look beyond their surface claims:

- They seem far more interested in the extrinsic rewards versus the intrinsic value of the role and the company's mission.
- They consistently demonstrate a "knower," not a "learner," mentality.
- For leadership hires, the candidate has limited examples of hiring and separation stories.
- They rarely, if ever, discuss past failures, and when they do, they place the blame on others.
- They can't explain career transitions in a clear, concise way.
- They embellish or overstate the impact of their accomplishments.
- They use "I" instead of "we" when sharing specific examples.

- They speak negatively about previous leaders and colleagues.

> **BUILDING A LEADERSHIP COMMUNITY**
>
> At Y Scouts, we don't post jobs, but we do maintain a robust leadership community. You can, too.
>
> We ask people to go online and fill out a questionnaire. Those questions touch on values and purpose: What brings you the most fulfillment in your work? What is your proudest accomplishment? What do you most value?
>
> Okay, we ask them to upload their resume, too.
>
> Often, a recruiting search starts by tapping into our leadership community and looking for possible candidates. People are especially happy to keep their information up to date in our community, because they know we are not going to spam them with opportunities that don't look like a serious match. Over time, we build trust with them, and they build trust with us.

YUP, PERSONAL LIVES MATTER

When you read about our methods, you might object that employers have no right to dig into personal lives, and that candidates should protect their personal lives from that digging.

Traditionally, people have been strongly advised to avoid personal details in interviews, assuming those topics are a turnoff to employers.

We think that tradition is dumb. If the candidate has primary care responsibility for a ninety-year-old mother, it will inevitably surface as a challenging factor at some point in their tenure. Why should everyone hide those details from one another? And hey, maybe you'd like to hire someone who feels responsible for their mother's well-being.

If it turns out this person must leave each Thursday at three to care for their mom and you're not okay with that, it will lead to trouble, fast. You both might as well find that out in an early interview. Don't wait until you've gone through the whole process, the candidate has quit another job, you've done an elaborate onboarding, and then during the third week, you say, "Hey, you can't just leave at three every Thursday." Your precious new hire might just say, "Well, then, I quit."

At Y Scouts, we believe it's far better to have meaningful discussions about the real issues that matter to people so everyone goes into a new relationship with open eyes. We can all be far more compassionate and empathetic with each other that way.

When you hire someone, guess what? You hire a whole person, not just their resume.

NOT WHAT THEY PREPARED FOR

When we go straight to personal issues in the recruiting process, our candidates actually love that we are breaking through the traditional boundaries. It's exhilarating and refreshing. It's not what they prepared for, and that's a good thing, too.

Max was for a time the membership chairman for the local chapter of the YPO, previously the Young Presidents Organization, a CEO/presidents group with a good deal of prestige. Naturally, he brought his very personal style to the interview process.

YPO interviews can be intimidating. Fifteen other CEOs sit around a table to decide whether someone should get into the group. Even hotshot CEOs get nervous in that situation and usually default into a sales-pitch-type presentation about their company and their accomplishments.

Max, being a Y Scouter, totally rearranged the questioning. He'd say, "In one minute, tell us about yourself, your family, and your business." Then he'd open it up for questions, and the first question would always be, "Tell us about your favorite family tradition, and why it's your favorite."

It was like flipping a light switch. People who felt comfortable about who they were relaxed and answered quickly. Others, who had rehearsed all the things they had planned to say, would turn bright red. You could practically hear them thinking, "Oh, hell, this isn't the type of interview I planned out."

Exactly.

MAKING THE SHIFT

Although informal initial inquiries are easier for us as a third party, a savvy company can do everything we do with in-house recruiters. Basically, it means changing your approach from reactive to proactive and making the shift to DNA-based conversations.

Use the Y Scouts Method, and you will be taking charge of your own future. You are only going to reach out to candidates who appear to be exciting, and because you are going to start with the person rather than the resume, you are going to end up with much better people in your life. If you're going to spend hours of every day with someone, don't you want to know whether you have chemistry?

Whether you will *like* them?

There's a famous Jim Rohn quote: "You become the aver-

THE COMPENSATION CONVERSATION

A salary offer should never come as a surprise. You should begin to address compensation early so you at least establish a range that might satisfy both parties. Nothing's worse than spending lots of time with a great person, only to discover that the two of you were thinking way differently on salary all along.

Until you develop a relationship, however, you probably won't get the full story on a candidate's current compensation package or understand all the factors in their decision process. Often, it's best to touch on the subject in the very first conversation, and then bring it up multiple times throughout your conversations.

You should also have frank conversations like "I would love to get a sense of where compensation lands in your order of priorities. Is it the number one decision point for you? Is it number three?" You may find that if your company offers a high sense of purpose and great alignment, a candidate will be willing to take less than what they would take to work somewhere else.

Other factors abound: flexibility, vacation, benefits, perks, level of influence. The candidate may have a spouse to consult, and plenty of other personal stakeholders, like kids who may have to switch schools.

As a hiring manager, you need to understand as many of these factors as possible and work through them transparently with the candidate. That takes time, and it takes effort. In the best of all possible worlds, everything will have been discussed so that by the time the offer is written out, everyone already knows what it will contain.

It's true that compensation negotiations often go more smoothly through a third party like our search firm. We remain unbiased and work to achieve the best possible outcome for everyone involved. After all, the lives of real people are greatly impacted by the work we do.

Always remember that every compensation negotiation is unique and must be handled on a case-by-case basis. Most of the time, the person the new hire will be reporting to is in the best position to close out the candidate negotiations.

Even more crucial than the pace or the nuances of negotiation are clear goals attached to a compensation package. At the leadership level, nearly all packages include incentives tied to achievements. But here's the good news: if you've done your advance work properly and have your list of success outcomes in hand, that part will come far easier, and the entire arrangement will make a good deal more sense down the line.

age of the five people you spend the most time with." If that's true, pick those five people wisely.

CALLING REFERENCES EARLY

Part of being proactive is actually doing the work to call references. At Y Scouts, we believe in calling lots of references as early as possible. In fact, as a search firm, we call references well before we send a candidate to interview at our client. We want to save both client and candidate all the trouble of interviewing if it turns out the guy or gal was a jerk at their last company.

You should make it your own best practice to call references as early as possible. It can be time-consuming, and if you put it off until after a decision has been made, it may not get done at all. Or the information may come too late to alter course.

Like everything to do with recruiting, making these calls is not easy. The information can be invaluable, but only if you ask the right questions, in just the right way.

The problem? Getting people to talk. Thanks to legal fears, references may not be allowed to directly share any information about a previous employee beyond title and dates of employment.

In any case, the best way to get people to talk is to be transparent about your intentions, making it clear that an honest conversation can help not just you but also the candidate to be sure a new job will be a good fit.

Sometimes, if you approach a reference very indirectly, you can find what you need. For example, you can call a previous supervisor and leave a message like, "Hi, I'm calling to do a reference on Brian Mohr. I'm hoping to hire him relatively soon. On a scale of one to ten, if you view him as a nine or a ten, please call me right away and let me know."

Hear nothing back, and everyone can draw their own conclusions.

You may even find it worthwhile to call (or message on LinkedIn, etc.) a candidate's successor at a previous company. The successor may know a lot, even if they never met the candidate, because they inherited the consequences of the candidate's work, and they've heard third-party opinions about what happened. Sometimes they feel free to talk in a way that supervisors won't. It's easy to find successors through company websites and sources like LinkedIn.

Our friend and mentor Ann Rhoades says she calls only the names candidates *don't* give her. Great advice, if you can get them to talk.

WHAT'S WRONG WITH RESUMES

No one would argue that resumes are unimportant. Trouble is, most hiring managers use the resume as the *primary* tool for understanding a candidate. Usually, it's the *only* tool used to decide whether the candidate gets a call. Resumes certainly offer some value in identifying table stakes, but if you use them as your primary filter, you are blinding yourself too much of what you need to know about a potential leader.

Common result? You find mediocre people. All-too-common result? You hire somebody totally wrong to do something really important.

Think of a resume as a long-distance rearview mirror. It looks in only one direction: backward. Way backward.

Even if the document happens to be truthful, you are looking at what someone *used to do* and may never want to do again.

ALL SMILES AND NO TEARS

Even an honest resume offers only the highlights of a career, with none of the failures. Think of it like Facebook or Instagram—all smiles and no tears. On a resume, as in social media, everything is great! No, really great!!! While in reality, of course, everyone stumbles and falls. Everyone has huge life struggles.

You need to learn about those struggles. Because only from the struggles do we understand how people became who they truly are as a person and what character they have built. Exactly none of that crucial information appears on a resume.

A resume is not a record of the person's career; it's only a record of the good stuff that happened in their career.

Or at least the good stuff they *say* happened in their career.

LET'S TALK EMBELLISHMENT

We figure about 50 percent of resumes are egregiously inaccurate—at all levels of candidates. Not only are resumes embellished, but people often hire professional resume writers who know how to embellish them in a spectacular manner.

A 2017 survey in *Inc.* magazine reported that about half of US workers, 46 percent, said they know someone who included false information on their resume.[7] A twenty-five-point jump from a 2011 survey. A full 38 percent of senior managers say their company has removed an applicant from consideration for a position after discovering he or she lied.

As for areas where employees tend to lie the most, it's job experience at 76 percent, followed by job duties at 55 percent, education at 33 percent, and dates of employment at 26 percent.

Another study says fully 85 percent of job applicants lie on their resumes.[8] But of course, who really knows?

From talking to colleagues overseas, we believe that embellishment occurs at a much higher rate in the US

---

7 Monica Torres, 2017. "Nearly Half of Us Are Lying on Our Resumes, Survey Finds." Accessed online, http://theladders.com/career-advice/nearly-half-of-us-are-lying-on-our-resumes-survey-finds

8 J.T. O'Donnell, "85 Percent of Job Applicants Lie on Resumes. Here's How to Spot a Dishonest Candidate." https://www.inc.com/jt-odonnell/staggering-85-of-job-applicants-lying-on-resumes-.html.

than anywhere else in the world. Why? Perhaps, like grade inflation, exaggeration has become almost expected here.

TECHNOLOGY ENCOURAGES EMBELLISHMENT

Earlier, we spoke a bit about the limitations of resume-scanning technology. Problem number one? Everyone now tailors their resume for scanning by each specific employer. Every single keyword you put in your job description will be added to a resume just before it's sent off to you. People feel forced into this strategy, as they know they will never get to the table unless they load the dice.

At the same time, the web has made it so absurdly easy to apply to hundreds of jobs simultaneously that employers—especially in the tech industry—have been pretty much forced into scanning just to cope with the volume.

It has all become a stupid, stupid game.

AVOIDING THE RESUME GAME

As you have seen, here at Y Scouts we try to do an end-run right around a resume.

Just to recap: (1) We don't post traditional job descriptions; we go hunting for our ideal candidates. (2) When we first talk to candidates, we do not reveal the specifics of the job we are discussing. This makes it really hard to tailor their answers and histories to the job. (3) That first conversation goes straight to purpose and values.

If you use this approach, believe us, when the candidate finally emails you their resume, you will read it with a far higher level of insight and understanding. It's also likely you will see right through any BS.

When we go out and recruit on behalf of a client, we do a lot of legwork to validate the data on resumes. But the best "investigation" often comes as a conversation with the candidate themselves. If you have a genuine chat that really digs into values, culture, and past behaviors, you will usually sense the mismatches between resume and reality.

You will just *know* that something is wrong.

BE CAREFUL WHEN LOOKING FOR "DOERS"

One caution before we close this chapter and move on to a discussion of the formal interview.

Whether reading through resumes or making targeted recruiting calls, we often hear our clients say they're looking for "a person willing to roll up their sleeves and execute." Or "a person willing to go down into the weeds and get their hands dirty if they need to. A real *doer.*"

LOOKING FOR THE TRUTH

Part of our job as search professionals is to validate the truth of resumes. But the sad fact is that unless you happen to have a personal relationship with the leaders of a candidate's previous employer, it's damn hard to do this. Companies are understandably leery of legal issues and will often stonewall any inquiries. It's worse when the parting came on bad terms.

Nasty resume scandals are always in the news. Some famous cases? In 2008, British chef Robert Irvine was fired from his show on the Food Network when it turned out he was not the guy who designed a royal wedding cake—he just attended the school where it was made and picked some fruit for the cake.

Marilee Jones taught at MIT for twenty-eight years before the college realized she'd never received any of the degrees she listed on her resume.

A few days after being named head football coach at Notre Dame, George O'Leary was forced to resign after lying about a master's degree and his own past as a player.[9]

The list goes on and on.

Recruiting companies have become part of the problem instead of the solution. Because they get paid on a "sale," recruiters have made an Olympic sport out of rewriting resumes and then loading the same BS onto the lips of candidates when they send them into interviews. Contingent recruiters have exaggerated the problem, because all their fees are contingent on candidates getting hired.

Everyone should remember that BS is bad for both companies and candidates—leading to trouble down the road, usually well after the recruiter has been paid. A candidate should write their own resume and be able to stand to it in an interview.

There's no question that a good leader gets stuff done. But often, these clients have a problem precisely because they're always looking for *doers* instead of *leaders*.

In chapter 1, we talked about the mistaken tendency to automatically promote the "most decorated" member of an existing crew to take over the role of captain when the old captain leaves.

The same syndrome must be avoided when recruiting outside your organization. The Y Scouts Method always looks for good captains, not just good crew members. Not even the *best* crew members. That's why you are asking all those open-ended questions in the first, informal conversation. It's why you are counting the skills on a resume only as table stakes. It's why you will focus on behavior-based questions in the more formal interview to come.

We once had a client who came to us in desperation after promoting a really outstanding engineer to lead an engineering group. The guy was definitely a *doer.* But for forty-five minutes, the client complained about how awful this engineer was in his new role. He approached leadership the same way he approached engineering:

---

9 Vivian Giang and Jhaneel Lockhart, "BUSTED: This Is What Happened To 10 Executives Who Lied About Their Resumes." http://www.businessinsider.com/9-people-who-were-publicly shamed-for-lying-on-their-resumes-2012-5#former-notre-dame-head-coach-lied-about-a-masters-degree-and-being-a-football-legend-in-college-when-he-never-even-played-a-game-5.

everything had an absolute answer, a formula everyone had to follow.

He *did* plenty. But he completely misunderstood people, and people were departing in droves.

Only when a company is led well does everyone execute and get things done. They do it because they understand and believe in the vision of the company. It's the leader's job to make sure everyone knows why they're tightening the bolts on the plane and where the plane's headed. He or she does not necessarily have to tighten the bolts personally.

In the next chapter, we will explore the attributes of a genuine leader more deeply. Then we'll use everything we've learned to create an Interview Guide for finally bringing that genuine leader into your company.

CHAPTER 6

Hiring for Leadership

In this chapter, we offer leadership essentials for business today. Then we explain how you should radically restructure your formal interviews to find those essentials in candidates.

Looking for a definition of leadership? As we write this book, just about everyone is being forced to rethink the whole idea.

The traditional concept of leadership stood directly on the notion of the corporate ladder. You started at the bottom, and by improving your performance and earning trust over time, you rose up in the ranks to increasing levels of responsibility. The theory was that if you were an amazing contributor on rung three, you could be trusted to move up to rung four. Ladders are all about good crew members becoming captains.

As we have learned, however, the very notion of the corporate ladder itself depended on the rigid systems devised by guys like Taylor and Weber. Why?

Because the ladder assumed that a clearly defined process of command and control will optimize results. Master the process, went the theory, and you have mastered success. Your job as you moved up? Push the people below just a little harder, toward incremental improvement. Make tiny tweaks in the process, and you have done your job.

Another assumption of the old-fashioned ladder: people on the higher rungs always better knew how to do things than people on the lower rungs. They had a broader view of the overall process, and process was king, so as you moved up you became kinglier. Indeed, as you climbed the ladder, your ego was expected to rise with your rank. An egotistical leader was pretty much required to maintain the command-and-control culture. If you didn't treat your employees like underlings, how would they know to stay in line?

The ideal most commonly held up for emulation was McDonald's. McDonald's had so perfected its processes that it could deploy restaurants at will and hire "trained monkeys" because no judgment was required at the lower levels to make the same cheeseburgers the same way everywhere. No judgment at all. Even if your company didn't flip burgers, you should be a McDonald's at heart.

Max really hates the famous 1986 book *The E-Myth,* along with its successor volumes, because author Michael Gerber idealized the concept of the franchise and its rigid organizational structures. He urged every business to pursue a trained-monkeys strategy, regardless of their industry, in the great hope of becoming the next McDonald's.

It was the model the last generation was told to love. But truth is, no one loved it. And to paraphrase Thoreau, the great mass of employees ended up working in quiet desperation.

SUCCESSFUL LEADERS ARE CONSCIOUS LEADERS

In this book, we talk a lot about leaders of large companies. But let's head into this chapter with the story of Adam Goodman of Goodmans Interior Structures. It's a medium-sized family business, and Adam is the third generation of leaders with the Goodman name. They sell office furniture.

After several years in his inherited position, Adam realized he wasn't passionate about office furniture. He saw that if he didn't feel a greater connection with his job, he would lead the company poorly—in fact, everyone he tried to lead would feel the exact same lack of purpose and meaning.

So Adam decided to start with an aggressive *learning* campaign. He surveyed every single customer and employee and asked them one simple question: "Why do you buy from us?" or "Why do you work for us?" From their responses, he learned the essence of why people cared about his company.

And it turned out that they did care.

Adam was amazed to find that the people involved, customers and employees alike, felt they were making a positive impact on the local community through their work. Yes, through office furniture. That furniture enabled people to work. Enabled nonprofits to function. Enabled significant good in the community.

Adam's realization was simple but magical. He saw that the products the company sold did not have to be the purpose of the company, and he used that insight to make himself and his employees more passionate. One result? When Goodmans went in to pull out old office furniture and install new stuff, they began donating all the older furniture to nonprofits. It became a quest, and Adam learned to become a true leader, a leader with purpose.

And guess what? Not only has his company been on fire ever since, but his success had absolutely nothing to do with Lean Six Sigma systems, more logical org charts, or anyone's climb up a ladder. But it had everything to do with leadership.

THE RESPONSIBILITIES OF A CONSCIOUS LEADER

A Taylorist or command-and-control leader would argue that their only responsibility is to create value for the shareholder or the investor. In fact, you see that kind of language in company mission statements all the time, and it's a basic tenet of old-style capitalism.

A conscious leader recognizes that although shareholder value is important, they must answer to many other stakeholders as well. A good company, a company with purpose, will create value for all those other stakeholders as well. The community. Their vendors and suppliers. Their customers. Their employees.

Yes, that means a conscious leader cares about making the lives of employees better, beyond the mere continued existence of their jobs. Sometimes that means waking up to the realities of the workplace.

One of our favorite stories about conscious leadership involves Bob Chapman, chairman and CEO of Barry-Wehmiller Companies. After a series of challenging years, Bob was desperate and needed to make some changes in his company, but he needed the passionate engagement of his employees to get those changes done.

Chapman was attending a wedding and had a simple but powerful realization as he watched a father walk his daughter down the aisle and give her away to her husband-to-be. He saw that every parent does their best to raise their children and provide them with the best life they can. And every single employee who worked for Barry-Wehmiller was someone's precious son or daughter.

At that moment, Chapman realized he was personally responsible for the well-being of every employee in his company. So he decided to treat them that way, moving forward from that moment. It led him to a broader vision, and he began preaching what he calls "truly human leadership." It made all the difference in getting his employees engaged and the company moving.

Another CEO we know used his own children as a reference point. He'd say, about dishonest or exploitative policies, "I wouldn't teach my son that kind of behavior; why would I teach or allow that kind of behavior in the workplace?"

Back in chapter 3, we gave the basic tenets of Conscious Capitalism. Anyone seeking leadership in today's marketplace should learn those tenets. But the values, the qualities, and the success goals you'd naturally want to teach your own children seem like a pretty good place to start.

Why would you care less about those values and goals when talking about your company?

THE THREE ELEVATED BEHAVIORS

At Y Scouts, we see our most-successful clients abandoning the notion of the corporate ladder with distaste, even scorn. They hire us to seek leaders who can take them to the future, not relentlessly perfect the processes of the past. The right leaders join the team and help ignite opportunities that the current team doesn't even know exist.

How do we get those people in place? We start with purpose and values alignment, and then we look for the Three Elevated Behaviors we see defining leadership today.

We spent years simplifying this list down to three. No kidding. We looked at hundreds of hiring outcomes from our searches in the past. We made long lists and whittled at them, because we realized that our clients could not focus on long lists, and neither could we.

Think of these behaviors like the legs of a three-legged stool: lose one, and you fall on your ass.

1. Learning relentlessly
2. Developing people
3. Driving results

What's not on this list? "Perfecting personal skills." "Devising systems." Why? Because the future of leadership belongs to the generalist, not the specialist.

Also not on the list: "being an egotistical jerk." Leaders today must put their egos aside and get other people involved. The idea that a leader knows more about everything than everyone down the line has become obsolete and counterproductive. In today's world, a good leader will help everyone process information together faster than anyone could alone—and the conscious leader is more than okay with that notion. He or she embraces it.

We are in a world that rewards servant leadership. Conscious leadership. If you are not looking for these Three Elevated Behaviors in a leader, you might be too focused on polishing the past.

LEARNING RELENTLESSLY

We put "learning relentlessly" at the top of our list, because as Adam Goodman discovered, it's the necessary engine to create the other two behaviors. What's at the center of most dysfunction in a company? Someone with a know-it-all mentality. Someone who lacks the desire to learn.

If a leader has no humility about what they know, they will not just resist new ideas but also miss the writing on the wall as the market changes. A leader who is not humble about their own knowledge will fail to develop others, and though they may drive results, they often drive the wrong results. They sometimes take the whole company over a Kodak-style cliff, albeit at top speed.

Just as importantly, by modeling the behavior of relentless learning, a good leader will inspire others to think and learn—necessary for the very survival of your company.

We all live in a world propelled more and more quickly by Moore's law—the exponential and accelerating development not just of chips but of everything. Think about the new world this way: change comes as slowly today as it will ever come.

In fact, let's repeat that another way so it sinks in: *change will never come as slowly as it comes today. In such a world, everyone must learn something new every single day. Maybe five new things a day.*

If success can no longer depend on the proven wisdom of the ladder, you should also now realize that it cannot depend on the wisdom of a process. Instead, success now depends on finding and developing the right people. Processes can be easily copied. Ladders fail quickly. Shit's going to change, and only people—not robots, not AI—can change with it.

Why has Southwest Airlines achieved impressive profitability, quarter after quarter, while so many other airlines have struggled? Southwest's process is an open book and can be copied by every other airline. There's no mystery about its planes, its seating methods, or its ticketing technology.

Southwest's success depends entirely on nurturing and developing its people on all levels in a fun manner. Its employees come first, even before its shareholders and customers. It knows that a successful enterprise is run by people who care about a purpose, a set of values, and true customer service. Not by trained monkeys.

Good leaders spend serious time developing other people until everyone has the knowledge to reach the leader's level. As the leader learns and develops, everyone must be brought along, or they will not be able to help anymore. We have concluded that people typically learn at about the same pace as they teach, almost to a one-to-one ratio.

DRIVING RESULTS

All the learning and people development on earth mean nothing without concrete results.

Fortunately, when you go out to recruit a leader, the results they achieved in the past are the easiest to measure. Do your homework, and your candidates cannot fake the way they came into a company, the revenue they drove, or the hiring results they achieved.

But if you really want to understand a leader's ability to drive results, you have to dig deeper than top-line revenue or profitability. You need to talk about expense reduction, reducing turnover, expanding market share, employee engagement, productivity increases, success in promotions, and hires. The works.

If you develop an effective Opportunity Profile and Interview Guide, you will have defined the results you need, and you can find out whether the behaviors exhibited in the past by your candidate have led to similar results.

Otherwise, you are batting blind.

RETHINKING THE FORMAL INTERVIEW

Ninety percent of formal interviews are conducted badly. Just gone about completely wrong. Seriously, we tear our hair out when we see how most people interview, even for the most important positions in their companies.

If you believe us about the Three Elevated Behaviors we have defined above, then you are probably beginning to see why your own interviewing skills have sucked so badly.

Let's improve that situation.

YES, YOU NEED TO PREP

A bad interview starts long before the interview. If you haven't properly defined the role or what success looks like in that role, then you really are "expecting the candidate to define success." If you haven't defined an ideal profile for a candidate, you're just "seeing what resumes come in." If you haven't thought about values or cultural alignment with your company's purpose, then you are "hoping she'll fit in." And if you expect the resume to tell you whether someone's a leader, you are truly just "hiring a resume."

Admit it: you usually just Google examples of good interview questions and best practices ten minutes before an interview, and then wing it.

No wonder you end up with leaders who cannot lead.

CREATE AN INTERVIEW STRUCTURE

Few companies create meaningful structures for an interview. But to achieve any kind of success, you simply must know what you're going to cover, who is covering what, and how you're going to score the interview results in the postmortem. Your interview structure must overcome the natural prejudices of interviewers for a single skill, a single type of background, or other criteria, which skews the result. Every decision about questions and goals should be deliberate, and stakeholders should have a say in each decision.

We strongly suggest the model of the Interview Guide created by Y Scouts, in which stakeholders are identified and brought into the process early. We will give you one example later in this chapter, and you will find more in appendix C.

But before we show you an actual guide, let's lay out some rules.

BUILD TRUST

Many interviewers overlook the importance of building trust at the beginning of a formal interview. They jump right in with a list of questions or pull out the candidate's resume to examine it with a magnifying glass. People open up far more quickly if you spend a little time creating a connection up front.

We recommend kicking off a meeting with something like, "We're super excited that you're here and that we're going to spend some time together. Our goal should be shared: arrive at an amazing decision that creates a better future for us both. We really need to get to know each other. Together, we need to figure out whether you're a good fit, whether our values align, and whether we'd all enjoy working as a team."

Then follow up with a little of that informal, personal stuff we discussed in the last chapter. "We've got a lot to cover, but before we jump right into the tough questions, let's just take a minute to get to know each other. After all, if this does work out, we're going to spend a lot of time together." Then ask about hobbies and how they like to spend their time outside of work.

If you make a speech about shared goals and then immediately go to "So tell me about a time you had to cut costs in your department," you've lost the ability to go back and get to know someone. The defenses go up, and the relationship can take an adversarial turn.

Instead of ending with the personal as an afterthought, start with the personal. That way, when you get to the "how to cut costs" stuff, the mask will be lowered, and you will inevitably get better results.

FOCUS ON BEHAVIORS, NOT SKILLS OR RESPONSIBILITIES

A good formal interview quickly moves the focus from *values* to *behaviors.*

Armed with your Opportunity Profile and its necessary success outcomes, you will have carefully formulated questions that will help you understand a candidate's prior behaviors as well as their potential contributions to your organization.

You already have their resume to tell you about their skills and responsibilities. They wouldn't be sitting here without table stakes. So don't waste your time.

Behavioral questions are not as open-ended as the more informal, values conversations you had earlier. You are now collecting specific data about *how someone previously acted in a role.* These stories will reveal how successfully a candidate might perform at your company. Here's an example of a well-formulated behavioral question:

> "Tell me about a time in your career when you broke a rule on behalf of an employee."

Your true goal is not to find out whether the candidate follows rules or what their level of responsibility happened to be. You want to learn whether they have an employee-first mentality and how they behave when a rule must be stretched.

Suppose their company gave only two weeks of vacation a year. You might hear about a time that an employee had already used up their two weeks but suddenly lost their mother and really needed two extra days to deal with that and go to the funeral. How was that handled? Listen carefully, and you may learn how this candidate will likely act in any non-standard situation regarding employees.

Here's another behavior-based question:

> "Tell me about a time you were faced with a really audacious goal but were constrained by resources. How did you respond? What did you do?"

If the candidate can't come up with any examples, maybe they've never faced the kind of challenges your company will throw at them. But if you're lucky, they'll roll into a story that tells you plenty: how they work with other departments, handle crises, respond to expectations, and get clever about resource allocation.

Once again, we're not talking hypotheticals. We're talking lived experience and exhibited behaviors. Here are a couple more examples of good behavior-based questions:

> "Tell me about a time when you were given really critical feedback from a supervisor that you did not immediately recognize as true. How did you react?"

> "Tell me about a time when you went head-to-head against a competitor to win a new client and you lost out due to price."

Does the candidate purposefully sidestep these kinds of questions? Do they stumble around to come up with examples? Bad sign.

In the back of your mind, you must always be thinking about the Three Elevated Behaviors: Does this person learn relentlessly? Develop people? Drive results? How are you going to find that out, based on their past behaviors?

As you have seen above, truth-seeking questions must be indirect. You can't ask, "Do you learn relentlessly?" But you can ask this:

> "Tell me about a time you shifted strategy based on a new trend and how you made that decision."

DIVIDE AND CONQUER

If you are interviewing a candidate for an important position, you already know they will have to undergo multiple interviews with multiple stakeholders. But too often, these interviews merely prove redundant, and the candidate simply perfects the same answer from interview to interview.

In your Interview Guide, consider dividing different kinds of questions among different interviewers. Know who is going to ask what, and you will get the broadest possible overview, plus all your interviewers will know that their piece of the puzzle matters.

NEVER ASK LEADING QUESTIONS

The most common interview mistake is the leading question. Basically, that means you telegraph the correct answer within the body of the question itself. If you say, "One of our values is integrity. Tell me about a time you showed integrity," you are pretty much guaranteed to get BS.

Of course, because most interviewers really *want* the candidate to be great, they subconsciously ask leading questions to *make sure* they get great BS.

To avoid this trap, you must ask a question that indirectly explores the candidate's integrity based on demonstrated behavior—for example, "Tell me about a time you had to make a tough business decision that was in support of a core value but may have had a negative short-term financial impact."

Or, "Tell me about a time you had to put your job on the line or make a major sacrifice in order to do the right thing."

Want to know whether the candidate focuses on developing employees? Don't ask a leading question like, "Do you believe in regular training programs for employees?" Ask, "What was the overarching company philosophy related to employee learning and development? And what was your philosophy?"

Without advance preparation, however, you will find it impossible to ask intentional, well-designed questions like these. No one can be that clever on the fly.

DON'T ASK YES-OR-NO QUESTIONS

You should avoid "yes or no" questions, which tend to be a waste of time. It's easy to ask a yes-or-no question by mistake, so here's a simple rule of thumb:

If the second word of your question is "you," you're probably asking something that boils down to yes or no. "Did you ever do X?" "Do you believe in Y?"

Questions like that tend to produce little useful information or conversation.

DON'T BE ADVERSARIAL

In spite of the indirectness of some inquiries, remember that the interviewer and candidate are not adversaries. It's stupid to head into an interview as a game of gotcha using trick questions or trying to ferret out inflated claims. Unfortunately, interviewers sometimes feel they have to do this because a resume could be filled with high-level BS.

Instead, spend your incredibly valuable interview time figuring out whether the candidate understands what leadership really means. If they don't, their impressive resume is either embellished or simply irrelevant, and you can stop wasting your time and theirs.

MAKE 'EM SHOW THEIR WORK

In the Y Scouts Method, truth-seeking does not mean exposing lies on resumes. It means getting past player stats to true behaviors and personalities. That means making the candidate show their work, just like on a high school math test.

Remember how if you just wrote X = 256 on your answer

sheet you'd get zero credit? If you didn't show every step in between, the teacher simply didn't know whether you understood the process of solving a problem. The same should be true during an interview.

If someone says they increased sales from $5 million to $10 million in a year, dig into that:

- What were the circumstances when sales were at $5 million?
- What did your team look like?
- Who contributed to those sales figures? How did you get to $10 million?
- Did you onboard or offboard people?
- Did you come up with new products? Sell them to the same or to new clients?
- Did you acquire a big new customer?
- Did you bring something to your teammates that helped them increase their share of wallet from existing clients?
- If I spoke to other people involved, what would they say about it?

A bullshitter will not be able to walk you through the steps of the entire process. As they do, you must be an active listener and ask follow-up questions until you have a complete understanding of that amazing $5-million-to-$10-million number.

Along the way, be sure to clarify numbers. If a resume says a candidate had fifty-two people reporting into them, was that actually two people reporting directly and fifty reporting to those two? If the candidate stumbles over answering questions like this or avoids them, you will learn something important about their character. Often, they will have repeated that fifty-two-reports number so many times that they will have begun to believe it themselves.

Showing their steps toward X = 256 uncovers the truth about the candidate, not just about the resume.

OWN THE INTERVIEW

Keep in mind that it's all too easy for a candidate to end up owning the interview. That means steering it in the direction of their personal agenda, not the company's. If a hiring manager or other stakeholder comes to an interview unprepared, they're likely to get rolled by a dynamic candidate.

Usually, of course, the interviewer does not come prepared. They're in the middle of a busy day, running from one appointment to another. They grab the candidate's resume and scan it ten minutes before the hour, and then attempt to wing a meaningful conversation.

Remember that the candidate will *always* have prepared in advance—and will be ready with answers to any crappy generic questions like, "Tell me about your greatest strength and your greatest weakness."

Just as unfortunately, an unprepared interviewer will be subject to their own prejudices instead of a clear set of values and success outcomes. Did the interviewer go to business school? Instead of focusing on the three behaviors, the whole damn hour might gravitate toward B-school memories.

SHUT UP AND LISTEN

Far too many interviewers talk too much. Talking a lot both masks the interviewer's unpreparedness and attempts to avoid the "awkwardness" of an interview—as if the goal were to have a "smooth conversation" instead of learning what makes the candidate tick.

Indeed, a manipulative candidate may focus on keeping the interviewer talking, because they know that people enjoy talking and will eventually give away the answers to all the questions as they ramble.

At Y Scouts, we try to keep our list of questions short and our own remarks brief. Ideally, we listen at least twice as much as we talk.

GROUP AND ONE-ON-ONE INTERVIEWS

In the summer of 2017, a nonprofit organization hired us to find it a CEO. A volunteer board of about thirty directors governed the organization, and they selected eight to serve on the selection committee. We created a Leadership Interview Guide because we needed to align the committee for the interview process. The guide specifically correlated to the success outcomes that existed in the Opportunity Profile.

We gave each member of the committee six different questions pertaining to a specific success outcome and told them to pick two or three to ask. Finally, we gave them a series of questions from which to choose for the Three Elevated Behaviors.

We recommend employing a mix of one-on-one and group interviews. People get more real when they engage in one-on-one conversations, but a lot can be learned in a group situation, simply because different people hear things differently.

Three is about the right number for a group interview, with a mix of genders. Five people might be a few too many, because then the candidate is going to be stressed out attempting to please and make eye contact with each person.

To make a group interview work, we strongly suggest having a ringleader. The ringleader opens up the conversation and works to maintain a relaxed atmosphere. If the conversation hits an awkward pause, a weird moment, or gets stuck on a point, the ringleader can grab the reins and move the conversation forward.

It's important to remember these meetings are about the candidate, and even though four or five people are in the room, it's the candidate who needs serious airtime. It might be a good move to huddle up beforehand and say something like, "Hey, team, quick reminder: we're here to learn about the person, not ourselves. If we do all the talking, there's a good chance we're not learning anything about the candidate."

We also suggest that if one person is leading a discussion on a certain topic, the other interviewers be the note takers. This allows for the person doing the talking to stay in the moment. You want to maintain a polite rigidity to the process.

In the case of this nonprofit, the three candidates we sent to the committee had already undergone a rigorous interview on values, completed by our search committee. Only those whose answers made us feel good about their candidacy progressed. In spite of our advance work, the interview committee also got a chance to explore values, purpose, and personal stuff.

RATING SYSTEM

In our Interview Guide for the nonprofit, we made sure to ask questions a candidate could not possibly prepare for in advance. That meant no standard BS questions about strengths and weaknesses. We were only interested in past behaviors that revealed whether a candidate could build a high-performance culture toward achieving this nonprofit's defined success outcomes.

We encouraged the selection committee to use a rating system to evaluate the candidates in their specific areas of competency. In this case, it was a one-to-five scale, five being the highest rating. At the end of the interview, everyone tallied up their scores in the different areas to see how these candidates ranked according to a similar measuring stick.

It's important to do postmortem meetings immediately after the interviews so the candidate will be fresh in everyone's minds. Otherwise, you are prone to lose context and details.

During these postmortems, an actual score may not be as important as the reason for that score. In a good postmortem, you will understand why a stakeholder interpreted something one way and another stakeholder interpreted it another. Within the dialogue, you will learn more about fit and more about the personality of the candidate as well.

Some people record interviews.[10] Not a bad idea, but it's important to introduce recording to the candidate in a way that keeps them loose. You can say something like, "Instead of my writing down what you say, I'd like to record it so that I can stay with you the whole time. I don't want you to get distracted by what I'm writing. I just want to allow us to have a conversation and not miss what we talk about so that I can reflect on it. Are you okay if I record this for my internal use only?"

SAMPLE INTERVIEW GUIDE: CHIEF EXECUTIVE OFFICER

Below is the full Interview Guide we created for this nonprofit's interviewing committee. It resulted in a super-aligned hire and great satisfaction among all the stakeholders. Study it closely, and you will see how the full process described in this book culminates in an interview truly focused on the Three Elevated Behaviors, "showing your work," success outcome alignment, and purpose/value alignment in a non-adversarial way.

10 Disclaimer: Always make sure you are following the legalities in your state when recording interviews.

Remember that this Interview Guide was created as part of the complete Y Scouts Method outlined in chapter 4. The candidates had already been through in-depth, rigorous interviews with Y Scouts, using our covert approach. Three members of the committee attended each interview and divided up the questions, which offer an intense focus on the Three Elevated Behaviors of leadership and the success outcomes we had defined with the client.

SUCCESS OUTCOME #1

Build a high-performance culture, leading mission-aligned team members toward the achievement of all objectives in the Strategic Plan. (Competency: Leadership)

Questions:

- What specific challenges have you encountered while reporting to a volunteer board? How did you work with your board to overcome the challenges?
- How have you balanced managing operations while remaining strategic? Have you ever focused too much on one aspect at the expense of the other, and if so, what did you learn?
- When have you made a hire that didn't work out? Did this shift your philosophy on hiring in the future?

- Describe a time when you have leveraged a very lean team to complete a major project.
- Describe a time you joined a company or started a new role and struggled to be effective at the beginning. How did you overcome this challenge?
- Describe a situation where you didn't take feedback well and why.

SUCCESS OUTCOME #2

Build a strategic resource development plan by the end of 2017 and implement the plan in 2018. (Competency: Resource Development)

Questions:

- When have you been responsible for securing corporate partnerships? Is there one you're especially proud of? Why?
- Describe a particularly beneficial partnership you have been able to secure and why you were successful in closing it.
- Describe a situation in which a relationship with a donor or sponsor has been strained and how you worked to restore it, successfully or not.
- Tell about a time you developed a ninety-day action plan. How much did you end up deviating from that plan, and why? What did you learn from this experience?

- How have you tracked donor retention and growth in the past?

SUCCESS OUTCOME #3

Enhance our brand position in the community, clearly establishing us as the best leadership development organization in the state. (Competency: Brand Ambassador and Community Involvement)

Questions:

- When have you had to be an ambassador for an organization?
- Tell me about a time you had to balance the demands of community involvement with those of your responsibilities outside the office.
- To what extent have you worked with the media?
- When have you spoken publicly, at conferences or otherwise?

SUCCESS OUTCOME #4

Continue to elevate the programmatic initiatives of our organization, resulting in life-changing leadership development training that is innovative, inclusive, and inquiring. (Competency: Program Innovation)

Questions:

- Tell about a time you stepped into a situation where the status quo was "we've always done it this way." How were you able to innovate beyond that kind of thinking?
- How have you leveraged technology in your previous roles?
- Given what you know of our programs, what kind of improvements might you consider?
- Describe a new program or procedure you implemented. How was it received? In retrospect, what might you have done differently?

SUCCESS OUTCOME #5

Engage the alumni base of our organization, making the most of their talent and community spirit to help move the organization and the state forward. (Competency: Alumni Relations)

Questions:

- Tell about a situation in which you've had to incorporate the input of a large constituency of interested parties, like an alumni group.
- How have you engaged alums of your organization?
- How have you used or implemented a method of tracking alumni? How effective was this method, and how might you apply it to our organization?

- How have you put in place processes and procedures related to gathering community feedback? What did these look like, and how did they impact your business?
- Describe a time when you received negative feedback on your organization. How did you respond?

EXCEPTIONAL LEADERSHIP TRAITS

(This section reminded all the committee members of their focus on the Three Elevated Behaviors and suggested related questions.)

Learns Relentlessly: In the twenty-first century, learning is more valuable than knowing as the world changes at a progressively faster pace. This individual has proof points in their life and their career that demonstrate curiosity and efforts to expand their knowledge base as often as possible. In addition, they are able to synthesize the information into their understanding of the world and its systems—they are open to changing their opinions and perspectives based on what they are learning.

Develops People: The best leaders inspire and improve the lives and performance of those around them. This leader will understand that without a strong team working together, these success outcomes are impossible to achieve. They will invest in their direct reports, providing coaching, mentoring, and guidance while also holding them to a high standard of performance.

Drives Results: Exceptional leaders are people who get things done. In a world full of leaders who talk a good game and present themselves with polish, the right leader will be someone who allows their accomplishments to do the talking. They will have a track record of success, having achieved challenging objectives and met clear stretch goals.

Questions

- Describe a new skill, concept, or methodology that you discovered or learned in the last year.
- Is there someone you have worked with whom you developed and mentored to the next level? Why do you believe you were successful in doing so?
- Describe a strategy you designed and implemented that led to significant, measurable growth for your organization.

THAT BEST POSSIBLE OUTCOME

We did our *fanatical preparation.* We worked damn hard to find *radical alignment.* At this point, we finally have the right to expect the *best possible outcome.*

What does a company with exceptional leadership look

like? It has more than success; it has the best chance of continued success because happy people work there. People eager to do their bests because they have a reason to do their bests. People who respect one another with a set of values. People who drive the right results because success has been defined in consonance with a company's core principles.

Importantly, these happy people have a model to follow every day—a genuine leader. That leader has not arrived randomly, self-selected through the lottery of a job board or the personal taste of an inexperienced hiring manager. That leader has not bullshitted their way in by fooling a resume scan or preparing their interview answers to suit a job description.

That leader has been hired on purpose.

Conclusion

Relentless Learning Revisited

"What worked well yesterday works less well today and likely won't work at all tomorrow."

—AUTHOR UNKNOWN

This book represents our best learning to date. But hopefully, like you and like the people you will hire, we know that our own learning must be relentless. We know that the Y Scouts Way must continue to evolve right along with the world we now occupy.

If we've accomplished nothing else, we hope you have learned that you cannot hire great people by constructing a beautiful website, writing a hyped-up careers page, and posting highly detailed job descriptions.

We hope you have learned that you must take a sincere and authentic interest in the personhood of the leaders you hire—what they love, the ideal environment in which they thrive, and the type of people they enjoy working with.

We hope you've learned that hiring is a full-contact sport. It involves a specific set of intentions, skills, and long-term commitment.

If you are a CEO or otherwise high up on the food chain, we hope you have learned that hiring leaders is not something you can delegate. Not something you can worry about only when the candidate is finally led into your impressive office.

Delegate something else to free up your time for this activity—anything else. Hiring leaders is primary to your strategic responsibility. Indeed, the best companies try to hire people with leadership qualities for every position, right down to ditchdigger. It's never just about skills. Everyone must focus on purpose and values. Anyone could be leading others one day, and we guarantee that your company will benefit enormously if even the ditchdigger is a relentless learner, tries to develop others, and drives results.

PLAYING OFFENSE AND DEFENSE

Way back in chapter 2, we introduced the underlying equation of the Y Scouts Way:

> *Fanatical Preparation + Radical Alignment = Best Possible Outcome*

As this book draws to a close, we'll add one more that you must never forget:

> *Individuals + Behaviors = Environment*

It's hard work to maintain a culture or to evolve a culture in a positive way. By bringing the wrong individuals into your company, believe us, you can screw up your whole company's environment, and screw it up damn quickly.

Hiring strategically means playing defense as well as offense. The only way to protect your culture and your team is to hire the right people with the right behaviors. In that sense, you as a hiring manager are responsible for the very survival of your team.

The Y Scouts Way is rigorous and methodical for a reason. We know you should always leave a leadership box empty, even for an uncomfortably long time, rather than hire the wrong person. We are consistently shocked at the brief and truly accidental hiring processes we see for leadership positions.

The chance that you can accidentally hire a great leader is extremely small.

YOUR DEFENSIVE LINE

Part of taking strategic responsibility for new hires will be your resolution to never go it alone. You must always remember that you cannot understand the right behaviors or the proper goals of a hire without involving multiple stakeholders.

To go back to our football analogy, you can think of your stakeholders as your defensive line. They will protect you from hiring someone who will not fit with your team and who may screw up your environment. They will identify issues you might never identify alone. They may even understand your company's values and culture better than you do.

Keep them involved.

NO SKIPPING OF STEPS

Remember, too, that to play defense and offense at the same time, you must know what you are looking for well before you set out to look for it. We have a defined a process for you to accomplish that. As of this writing, we know of none better.

If you have read diligently, you know you cannot skip any of the steps in this book if you want that best possible outcome. Start with values and purpose. Define the role. Define the ideal candidate. Set the table stakes. Look for behaviors.

Always remember that the process will not be easy. Nothing this important ever turns out to be easy.

CREATING THE HABIT

Getting good at hiring is a lot like staying in shape and keeping a good diet. You can't do it for a short period of time and expect serious results. And there are no quick fixes.

Look at good recruiting as a cumulative process. A lifelong process. The circumstances are always going to change, but you have to stay with it. If you want to remain healthy and fit, you've got to eat well, adjust your diet, and continue to work through injuries to stay in shape. The same is true for your company and its hiring practices.

This book is not a little magic pill. It's a discipline.

It's an invitation to up your game so you make better hires every time from here on out. We challenge you to think of anything more important to your business life.

ACCEPTING YOUR MISSION

Our great hope is that just by picking up this book, you have already proven yourself a relentless learner. That you have set out to do this thing in a new and better way.

Our great fear is that you will put this book down and not make a change. That next time you're staring at an open position on your org chart, you will just post a damn JD and hope for the best.

Instead, look to yourself for the same qualities you seek in the people you hire: Learn. Develop. Drive results. To hire a conscious leader, you must also become a conscious leader.

Make the leap.

Appendix A

Sample Opportunity Profile

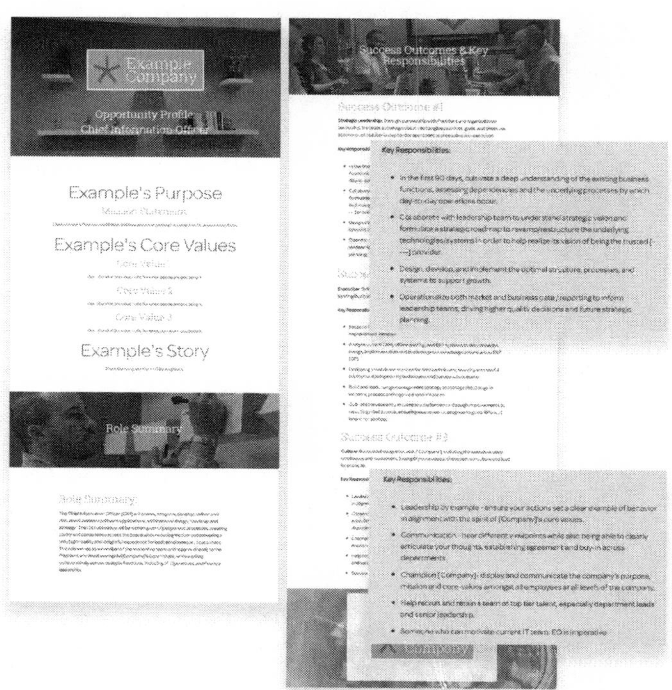

Appendix B

Ideal Candidate Profile

Example's Purpose

Example's Core Values

Core Value 1

Core Value 2

Core Value 3

Example's Story

Role Summary:

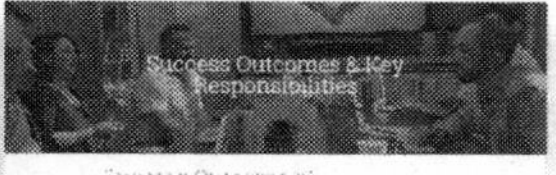

Success Outcome #1:

As Evidenced By:

- At least 15 years of professional success in roles of increasing responsibility, at least 10 years of which will include leadership of high-performance teams. (Mark not hung up on this - culture is more important***)
- Proven track record of leading process integration, implementation, and change management.
- Specific examples of driving winning solutions with a positive outlook; taking responsibility, learns from failure and embraces uncertainty.
- Sense of urgency; makes it happen and does the right thing; must be a team player who owns issues and acts and strives to be the best.
- Evidence of a strong working knowledge of data analysis and performance/operation metrics; will be practiced in data-focused decision-making and problem-solving.

As Evidenced By:

- Proven examples of selecting and implementing new ERP and/or Operating systems.
- Technically proficient in Microsoft Azure, SQL, Sharepoint, Great Plains (GP), Dynamics 365, ERP, CRM and SalesForce.
- Deep understanding of project management methodologies and best practices. PMP and/or Six Sigma certification preferred.
- Experience working with IT teams to develop a continuous improvement program for all IT hardware, software and operating systems to maximize efficiency and cost savings.

Appendix C

Sample Interview Guides

CIO Interview Guide
Example Company
Success Outcome 1
Questions:
Success Outcome 2
Questions:
Success Outcome 3
Questions:
Alignment to Example Company's Core Values:
Live life as hard as you work.
Treat people like they're part of the family.

Align to the Y Scouts Leadership Model

About the Authors

Max Hansen is a hiring process strategist who partners with CEOs, presidents, and other executive hiring managers to grow their businesses by hiring A-players. After spending nearly two decades successfully hiring tens of thousands of leaders in almost every industry, Max's true passion is up-leveling everyone's hiring game with purpose.

Brian's career to date has been a learning-based journey with an intense focus on people, purpose, values, culture, leadership, and advocating capitalism as a force for good. Brian is on the global board of trustees of Conscious Capitalism,

Inc., and a member of the board of directors of the Better Business Bureau of the Pacific Southwest. Brian's most important and cherished responsibilities are being the lucky father to his two daughters, Taylor and Riley, and the proud husband to his wife, Jackie. In his spare time, you'll find Brian practicing guitar and enjoying an occasional game of Texas Hold'em poker.